PIKE RIVER:
THE CRIME AND COVER-UP

The fight for the truth about how and why 29 workers died
in New Zealand's 2010 Pike River Coal mine disaster

Tom Peters

Articles and commentary from the World Socialist Web Site

Mehring Books
April 2022 (Reprinted: June 2022)
Printed in Auckland, New Zealand

Contact the Socialist Equality Group (New Zealand):
Email: socialistequalitynz@gmail.com
Facebook: /socialistequalitynz
Twitter: @SEGNewZealand

Printed in New Zealand by BookPrint

Cover photo by Richard Healey: roadside memorial to the Pike River 29

About the author: Tom Peters has been a regular writer for the *World Socialist Web Site* since 2008. In 2010, he joined the Socialist Equality Group, the New Zealand supporters of the International Committee of the Fourth International. He writes on New Zealand politics, workers' struggles, the fight against war, the COVID-19 pandemic, historical and cultural issues, and on Asia and the Pacific region. He has been writing about the Pike River mine disaster since November 2010.

Contents

Appendices

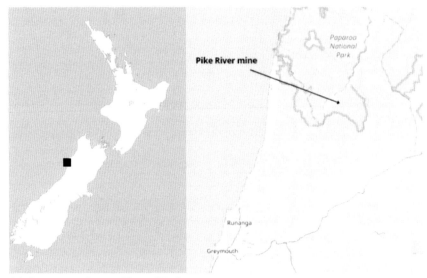

Pike River mine in Paparoa National Park. (Sources: Wikimedia Commons; openstreetmap.org, CC BY-SA 2.0)

Introduction

The Pike River underground coal mine, located in the Paparoa mountain ranges on the West Coast of New Zealand's South Island, exploded on November 19, 2010. Thirty-one workers were underground at the time and only two escaped with their lives. Three more explosions tore through the mine on November 24, 26, and 28, leaving no hope of any more survivors. The bodies of 28 men and one 17-year-old boy have never been recovered.

The disaster, and the revelations that followed about conditions in the mine, profoundly shocked working people throughout New Zealand and the world. Despite initial attempts by politicians, the media and union bureaucrats to claim that there was "nothing unusual" about the mine, it soon became clear that the 29 deaths were preventable and were the outcome of profit-driven corporate decisions. Yet, to this day, no one has been held to account.

Pike River was New Zealand's first major private coal mine developed in the 21st century to supply the world market, in particular the burgeoning

Asian steel industry. It was the flag-bearer for privatising the coal industry, and marketing it globally, and had been set up to break the dominance of the state-owned mining company, Solid Energy. Before a shovel of coal had been dug, it had become the best performer on the stock exchange, listing as one of the country's 50 largest corporations with a market capitalization of NZ$400 million. Under pressure from shareholders and creditors to speed up its operation, Pike River Coal (PRC) began production before the mine had been properly commissioned, cut costs on safety, and gambled with the lives of its workers.

This book analyses the causes of the disaster, including the pro-business deregulation of safety by successive governments, and the complicity of state agencies, regulators, and the trade union bureaucracy. The unions functioned as an accomplice to PRC, ensuring that the mine continued to operate despite the company's illegal and life-threatening practices. The book also explains how governments and the judicial system shielded PRC's managers and board members and sought to prevent a proper investigation of the mine.

The material reprinted here is part of the campaign waged by the Socialist Equality Group (SEG) and the *World Socialist Web Site* (WSWS) to mobilise the working class, in New Zealand and internationally, to join the fight to uncover the full truth about what happened at Pike River. The SEG supported the majority of the families of the Pike River victims, who opposed the Labour Party-led government's decision in 2021 to shut down the manned re-entry of the mine.

The families' determined struggle for truth brought them into conflict with the entire political establishment, as well as the union bureaucracy. Most of the media and the government's upper middle class, pseudo-left supporters sought to bury the issue of Pike River.

By the end of 2021, Jacinda Ardern's government had permanently sealed the mine, preventing the recovery of human remains and the examination of forensic evidence. This was done in the face of growing opposition from working people in New Zealand and internationally.

In November 2010, the WSWS responded immediately to the disaster. An article published three days after the first explosion opposed the united efforts of the National Party government, opposition Labour MPs, media pundits, and the Engineering, Printing and Manufacturing Union to whitewash Pike River's safety record. The WSWS stated: "Far from being a random or natural catastrophe, the information that is emerging points to the explosion at the Pike River Coal mine, like recent mine disasters in the US, Chile and China, being the result of entirely man-made factors: the compromising and sacrifice of miners' health and safety on the altar of corporate profit."[1]

The WSWS held a public meeting at Victoria University of Wellington on December 16, 2010, to discuss the political lessons of Pike River. It placed the events in the context of the deepening crisis of the global capitalist system, following three decades of pro-business deregulation, culminating in the financial crisis of 2008, which intensified the cut-throat competition for raw materials and markets. SEG member and WSWS writer John Braddock argued that Pike River and similar disasters showed the urgent need for a socialist party capable of uniting workers internationally to end capitalism. This had become "literally a life and death question for the working class."

The truth of this statement was tragically confirmed again in the February 22, 2011, Christchurch earthquake, in which 115 people lost their lives in the collapse of the cheaply and unlawfully constructed CTV building. This book includes an article written for the 10th anniversary of this horrific event, for which, as with Pike River, no one has been held accountable.

The sacrifice of workers' lives for profit has reached horrifying proportions during the COVID-19 pandemic. Over 20 million people have died worldwide (according to *The Economist*'s April 2022 estimate) because capitalist governments refused to implement the public health measures necessary to eliminate the deadly virus.

The Ardern government abandoned its elimination policy in October

---

1. "New Zealand: 29 miners still missing after underground explosion" https://www.wsws.org/en/articles/2010/11/mine-n22.html.

2021, to the dismay of scientists and ordinary people in NZ and throughout the world. Bowing to the demands of big business, New Zealand's Labour-Greens coalition joined other governments in insisting that the virus must be allowed to circulate throughout the country, and that the population must accept more deaths and severe illnesses as inevitable.

The unions have enforced the reopening of schools and nonessential businesses. As a result, hundreds of thousands of people have been infected with the Omicron variant, and severely underfunded hospitals are being forced to cut back on other services to accommodate COVID patients. By June 2022, there were more than 1,000 COVID-related deaths, up from 59 at the end of 2021.

With millions of workers now exposed to a potentially lethal virus because of deliberate and criminal policy decisions, the lessons of Pike River have a burning relevance. This book argues that workers can only defend their safety and their lives by building new organisations: rank-and-file safety committees, controlled by workers themselves and independent of the pro-capitalist unions. This task is inseparable from the struggle to establish the political independence of the working class from Labour and its allies, by building a new party based on the socialist and internationalist perspective and principles of Trotskyism—the New Zealand section of the International Committee of the Fourth International.

This book contains articles originally published on the WSWS, and three speeches delivered at a public webinar organised by the SEG on May 8, 2021. For this publication, many of these pieces have been edited; some shortened, to minimise repetition, and others significantly expanded. The analysis draws upon dozens of articles published by the WSWS since November 2010, including interviews with members of the victims' families.[2]

---

2. The full archive of the WSWS's articles on Pike River is available here: https://www.wsws.org/en/topics/event/2010-pike-river-mine-disaster

There are also contributions from Bernie Monk, whose son Michael died in the mine, and Michael's sister Olivia Monk, both of whom demand that the underground investigation continue.

A speech by Terry Cook, a writer for the WSWS and member of the Socialist Equality Party in Australia, reviews the 1994 Moura mine disaster and its aftermath. Cook's speech, delivered at the May 2021 webinar, underscores that the experience of Pike River is not exceptional but was part of a chain of similar disasters internationally.

The Appendices include: a statement from the E tū union making clear its support for the Ardern government's sealing of Pike River; letters from WSWS readers in support of the Pike River families' fight for truth; and a letter from UK mines rescue expert Brian Robinson addressed to the NZ government's Pike River Recovery Agency, denouncing the sealing of the mine. Two earlier WSWS articles are also included: an initial response to the findings of the Pike River royal commission in November 2012, and a report on the October 2017 Supreme Court hearing where families sought a judicial review of the decision not to charge PRC chief executive Peter Whittall.

This book could not have been written without extensive collaboration with John Braddock and with members of the WSWS Editorial Board in Australia. Several family members of the Pike 29 contributed invaluable information and perspective, particularly Dean Dunbar, Bernie, Kath and Olivia Monk, Carol and Steve Rose, Gordon Dixon, Ben Joynson, Malcolm Campbell and Cloe Nieper. Electrical engineer Richard Healey, who has conducted extensive independent research on Pike River, provided critical information. The author also wishes to thank Fiona Kidman, Brian Robinson and Maan Alkaisi.

This work is dedicated to the 29 workers who died in Pike River, and to the millions of workers throughout the world whose lives are placed at risk by governments, big business, and the corporatist trade unions.

Workers killed at Pike River:

Conrad Adams, 43
Malcolm Campbell, 25
Glenn Cruse, 35
Allan Dixon, 59
Zen Drew, 21
Chris Duggan, 31
Joseph Dunbar, 17
John Hale, 45
Dan Herk, 36
Dave Hoggart, 33
Richard Holling, 41
Andrew Hurren, 32
Koos Jonker, 47
William Joynson, 49
Riki Keane, 28
Terry Kitchin, 41
Samuel Mackie, 26
Francis Marden, 41
Michael Monk, 23
Stuart Mudge, 31
Kane Nieper, 33
Peter O'Neill, 55
Milton Osborne, 54
Brendon Palmer, 27
Ben Rockhouse, 21
Peter Rodger, 40
Blair Sims, 28
Josh Ufer, 25
Keith Valli, 62

A placard used in the families' July 2021 protest highlights the death toll from successive New Zealand disasters, for which no one has been held to account: the 1896 Brunner mine disaster, the 1967 Strongman mine disaster, the 1979 Air New Zealand plane crash at Mount Erebus in Antarctica; the 1995 collapse of a scenic viewing platform at Cave Creek; the 2010 Pike River disaster; and the CTV building collapse in the 2011 Christchurch earthquake. (Source: "Pike 29 Fight for Justice" Facebook page)

A memorial with the names of the Pike River 29, and Joseph Dunbar's memorial stone in the foreground. (Photo by Dean Dunbar)

Political lessons of the Pike River disaster

This is an expanded version of a speech given at the Socialist Equality Group's public webinar on May 8, 2021, titled "Ten years after the Pike River mine disaster: Political lessons of the fight for the truth about the deaths of 29 men."

It has been more than a decade since the disaster at Pike River mine claimed the lives of 29 workers. Speaking on the tenth anniversary of the disaster on November 19, 2020, Prime Minister Jacinda Ardern declared that the Labour government was "very close to fulfilling" its pledges to provide "closure" for the families of those who died. She said her government would "promote accountability for the tragedy and to help prevent future mining tragedies."

Despite repeated promises over the past decade, by National Party and Labour governments, that they would retrieve bodies and tell the full truth about what happened at Pike River, the opposite has been the case. To date, the state has held no one accountable for the deaths, and the government is preparing to seal the bodies, and crucial evidence, within the mine.

A disaster caused by capitalism

Pike River Coal's management sent men underground, day after day, into a mine that they had been warned was extremely dangerous, and that could have exploded at any time. They gambled with men's lives for the sake of profit. This criminal operation was assisted by the government regulators and the Engineering, Printing and Manufacturing Union (EPMU), which had about 70 members working at Pike River and did nothing to protect them.

The 29 deaths were not an unavoidable or random accident, just as the overwhelming majority of the millions of deaths from the coronavirus pandemic were not necessary or inevitable. We are living through a global catastrophe, not because the coronavirus can't be contained and beaten, but because governments and big business have refused to take the necessary measures such as lockdowns, factory and school closures, mass testing, border quarantine, and the isolation of positive cases.

Governments have prioritised production and profit over human life, starkly revealing the real, brutal f ace of capitalism. In October 2020, UK Prime Minister Boris Johnson reportedly blurted out during a meeting with his inner circle: "No more f***ing lockdowns, let the bodies pile high in their thousands!" That is the attitude of the British ruling class and its counterparts globally. The *BMJ*, formerly the *British Medical Journal*, in a February 2021 editorial, characterised the response of governments internationally to the pandemic as "social murder."

Governments would not be able to get away with this murderous policy without the collaboration of the trade unions. There is not one country where these organisations have mounted a campaign to defend workers from the virus or from the destruction of their living standards.

Likewise, Pike River reveals the real character of these organisations. They are thoroughly undemocratic and led by a privileged upper-middle-class bureaucracy, who are close to the Labour Party and whose interests are intertwined with those of big business. They oppose strikes and any action that could disrupt businesses, because that would also impact on the material interests of the well-paid union bureaucrats themselves.

Let us review what happened at Pike River. The causes of this disaster include the sweeping deregulation of the mining industry by successive governments. In 1992, the National Party government abolished worker-elected safety check inspectors. These were workers authorised to clear a mine if they considered it dangerous.

The number of mining inspectors employed in the Department of Labour (DoL) plunged during the 1990s from about 20 people to just one specialist mining inspector at the time of the disaster, who was responsible for thousands of mines and quarries throughout New Zealand. Companies were allowed to self-regulate and Pike River operated with minimal and ineffectual oversight.

Experts warned that deregulation would lead to a disaster. Billy Brazil, a former mining inspector, wrote in a submission to the government in 1995: "Due to the abolition of specific safety legislation, and [...] bureaucratic incompetence, mine safety in New Zealand today is held together with a rubber band." He called on the government to "act immediately to restore our legislation before another Kaitangata Disaster," referring to the 1879 explosion that killed 34 miners.[3]

After Helen Clark's Labour Party government was elected in 1999 it did not reverse any of National's attacks, and the unions did not mount any campaign to force the government to act.

The destruction of mining regulations was part of a sweeping pro-business agenda, launched by Prime Minister David Lange and Finance Minister Roger Douglas' Labour government in 1984. It privatised telecommunications and prepared other industries for privatisation, including railways and forestry by transforming them into profit-making enterprises and sacking tens of thousands of workers. The state-owned coal mines were restructured along these lines, with Huntly and the West Coast losing hundreds of jobs.

National protections and subsidies for agriculture were abolished, which devastated many farmers. Fees were introduced for healthcare and tertiary education. The Goods and Services Tax was introduced, while taxes for the rich and for corporations were slashed.

These brutal attacks on the working class led to soaring unemployment and social inequality that New Zealand has never recovered from.

The 1980s Labour government was seen as a model for right-wing restructuring, which mirrored what was happening under President Reagan in the United States, Margaret Thatcher in Britain and the Hawke/Keating Labor government in Australia. In response to the globalisation of production, governments went about scrapping any restraints on profit making, including

---

3. "Pike River: Inspector warned of explosion," *New Zealand Herald* December 11, 2010.

health and safety red tape.

All of this was done with the collaboration of the unions. These organisations, internationally, transformed themselves into industrial policemen. They worked with the state and big business to ensure orderly redundancies, suppress strikes, and to defend the ability of their country's businesses to compete and make profits on the world market.

The deregulatory frenzy affected the construction industry, leading to thousands of unsafe and leaky buildings. The cheaply built and unstable CTV building, constructed in Christchurch in 1986, collapsed in seconds during the earthquake less than three months after Pike River, killing 115 people. As with Pike River, no one has been held accountable for this avoidable tragedy.

These were the conditions in which Pike River developed during the 1990s and 2000s, under National and Labour governments, and eventually opened in late 2008. Mining companies were now competing against rivals internationally with much lower wages and operating costs.

Mine workers in every part of the world suffered deaths, sickness and injuries as a result of the race to the bottom. Pike River was part of a wave of mine disasters in 2010, including in China, Turkey, Chile, Russia and the United States. In an event with many similarities to Pike River, the Upper Big Branch mine in West Virginia exploded on April 5, killing 29 men. Massey Energy had failed to properly ventilate the mine, and the company's blatant disregard for safety coincided with a speed-up in production and a cost-cutting drive. Over the previous 18 months, the mine had more than 600 safety violations, including for ventilation plans, escape routes and coal dust control, but the Mine Safety and Health Administration never sought to close it down.[4]

Likewise, to cut costs, Pike River's leadership committed so many egre-

---

4. Massey Energy CEO Don Blankenship was convicted on minor charges and spent one year in prison. Blankenship, the first coal executive convicted over a disaster in the US, also received two years' pay and a $12 million pension. See: "Former Massey Energy CEO Don Blankenship released from prison," May 13, 2017, https://www.wsws.org/en/articles/2017/05/13/blan-m13.html

gious safety violations, it is not possible to mention them all here. The mine had no suitable second egress, as required by law. It had grossly inadequate methane monitoring, ventilation and drainage systems. Its main ventilation fan was installed underground, which is never done in underground coal mines anywhere in the world because of the dangers it poses.

The royal commission in 2012 documented many of these facts, many of which were already known by the DoL and the EPMU.

Masaoki Nishioka, a Japanese hydro-mining expert who did some work for Pike River, told the commission that he warned chief executive Peter Whittall, manager Doug White, and others about the dangerous lack of ventilation. He was ignored, and he quit one month before the explosion, because, he said, "I felt the mine would explode at any time."

Many similar complaints were made. Shift supervisor Dene Murphy submitted an incident report to his superiors in June 2010 highlighting "very inadequate ventilation" and saying safety procedures were not properly enforced. On October 21, Murphy filed another report, saying: "Get the dam ventilation sorted out so we can cut coal. This ventilation issue has dragged on for 2½ years!!!"

The mine owners decided that to bring the mine up to standard would have been too expensive. Pike River had already borrowed tens of millions of dollars from its largest shareholder NZ Oil and Gas, and from the Bank of New Zealand.

Due to cost overruns and breakdowns, the first shipment of coal was only sent in February 2010. The board introduced a $10,000 incentive for workers to produce 1,000 tonnes of coal by September 24, speeding up production under conditions where the main fan had not yet been commissioned. The royal commission found that "methane levels rose to explosive levels in the return twice in the days leading up to this deadline."

The DoL could have shut the mine down long before it exploded. Harry Bell, a former chief inspector of coal mines, was alarmed when he learned about several underground methane gas ignitions in November 2008. Whittall, then

17

general manager, brushed aside the incidents, telling the *Greymouth Star* on November 20 that the fires were quickly put out and the mine had "state of the art electronic, real time monitoring" of gas levels—a claim that was later proven false.

Bell told the DoL at the time: "Stop them bloody mining until they fix the ventilation." In his testimony to the royal commission in July 2011 he explained he had said "it was nonsensical, madness... to go through the fault with a single drive entry because of the gas risk... I told the [DoL] inspector that he could tell [the] mine's staff that I was the whistle blower, that I was furious and alarmed that this had happened after the warnings and discussions."

The warnings were ignored. The DoL sent letters to the company expressing concern but did not issue a prohibition notice or prosecute anyone.

The role of Labour and the EPMU

Two days after the first explosion at Pike River, the Labour Party's MP for the West Coast, Damien O'Connor suggested that Pike River Coal wasn't necessarily to blame. He told TVNZ that the mine was run according to "the very best international standards." He said the disaster was "one of these things that the West Coast, unfortunately, has had to get used to over the years. We're an economy and community based on primary production and mining, and from time to time, unfortunately, in spite of our best efforts, sometimes these disasters happen."[5]

Two years later, after the damning evidence revealed by the royal commission, O'Connor tried to defend his party's record, but only revealed the indifference of Labour and the union bureaucracy to mine safety. O'Connor told TV3's "The Nation" on November 10, 2012 that he now felt "guilty" he had not done more to prevent the tragedy. He admitted that Billy Brazil had warned

---

5. The transcript of O'Connor's comments to TVNZ on November 21, 2010 can be read here: https://www.scoop.co.nz/stories/AK1011/S00404/q-a-interviews-west-coast-based-mps.htm

him that deregulation would "result in a massive mine disaster because deregulation has done that through the world time and time again." Even after two deaths at the ROA and Black Reef mines in 2006, recommendations to improve safety were ignored by the Labour government. Admitting he had not pushed to change the law after Labour won the 1999 election, O'Connor blamed the DoL, saying it had "supported deregulation."

O'Connor sought to cover up the role played by the EPMU in suppressing opposition to deteriorating mine safety. Asked whether Labour had received any advice from the EPMU to change the law, O'Connor avoided answering directly. He defended the EPMU, telling TV3 "the coal miners themselves... weren't demanding of their own union that things should change." He declared that "the whole community, when it knew that things weren't quite right at Pike River, should have been more forceful." In other words, according to O'Connor, the miners and wider working class were collectively responsible.

Similar statements appeared in the media, blaming workers for "allowing" and "tolerating" deregulation of safety standards.[6] The aim was to divert attention and shift blame away from Labour and National's policies, enforced by the union bureaucracy, which allowed companies to put profit ahead of safety.

The EPMU had the power to stop production at Pike River by going on strike, but it did nothing. The union's leader at the time of the explosion was Andrew Little, who was also President of the Labour Party. In 2014 he became the Labour Party's parliamentary leader, until he was replaced by Jacinda Ardern shortly before the 2017 election. He is now the minister responsible for Pike River, tasked with shutting down the underground investigation.

On January 18, 2017, Little rejected growing criticism of the EPMU's role, telling *Stuff*: "I absolutely stand by our track record on improving health

---

6. In the *Dominion Post*, Sean Plunket echoed O'Connor, writing that "the miners themselves... were part of the problem" ("We all share blame for Pike River," November 10, 2012). Fellow columnist Dave Armstrong claimed that "four million New Zealanders... happily tolerated" deregulation ("Pike River: Why we are all guilty," November 12, 2012).

and safety both at Pike River and in mining generally. ... Our union and its members led a walk-out on health and safety grounds just weeks before the fatal explosion."

The walk-out, the only industrial action ever taken at the mine, was initiated by a group of about 10 miners. One worker telephoned a union representative and said they were concerned about the lack of emergency equipment. According to former Pike River worker Brent Forrester, who spoke out about the incident following the disaster, "The union representative said, 'I believe you should come out, but it's your call.'" This advice was the full extent of the EPMU's involvement.[7]

Before the disaster, the union said nothing about the walk-out publicly. Pike River Coal was allowed to continue lying that it had an impeccable safety record. The union later revealed to the royal commission that it also knew about the gas ignitions in 2008 and the lack of a proper emergency exit. But the EPMU ensured that, day after day, workers kept going underground despite the immense dangers.

In one of its 2017 election campaign ads, Labour declared that Little "supported the Pike River families from day one – and still does." In fact, on the *World Socialist Web Site* in the days after the disaster, we pointed out that Little was rushing to defend the company before the dust had even settled.

Little told Radio NZ three days after the first explosion: "Every mine on the West Coast takes great care when it goes into production and I don't think Pike River is any different to that. They've had a good health and safety committee that's been very active. So, there's been nothing before now that's alerted us to any greater risk of this sort of incident happening than at any other time." He similarly told the *New Zealand Herald* that the company had "an active health and safety committee; the union's well-represented on it. ... There's nothing unusual about Pike River, or this mine, that we've been particularly

---

7. "Sunday," TVNZ, December 5, 2010. See also: "Former Pike River Coal miner hits out at lack of mine safety," https://www.wsws.org/en/articles/2010/12/mine-d10.html

concerned about."[8]

The union was covering up the conditions, over which it had presided, that led to the disaster. Little's comments allowed the *Dominion Post* to run a front-page article on November 26 criticising "wild" rumours that the mine was not safe. "Any suggestion of obvious or known safety lapses does not find traction with unionised staff or union leader Andrew Little," it said.

Politicians and judicial system protect Pike River management

Government and opposition parties alike rallied to defend Pike River Coal and its chief executive Peter Whittall, who was treated as practically a hero in the media.

On November 25, for example, Green Party MP Kevin Hague said in parliament: "I will single out Peter Whittall... I will take this public opportunity to convey the Green Party's thanks, our enormous sympathy, but also our tremendous respect for the integrity, responsibility, and compassion that he has unfailingly shown." Jim Anderton, leader of the Progressive Party and former leader of the pseudo-left Alliance, made a similar comment, saying Whittall had "shown calm, intelligent leadership and great strength at a difficult time."

These "left" politicians were indistinguishable from right-wing ACT Party leader Rodney Hide, who thanked Whittall "for your leadership, your courage, your honesty, and your humanity."

Echoing these sentiments, the *New Zealand Herald*'s Phil Taylor gushed on November 27 that Whittall had "a passion for the industry and its people, a natural affability and rare presenting skills," and had "delivered beyond expectation" following the disaster.

At an official remembrance service on December 2, Whittall spoke along

---

8. Radio NZ, "Miners' union demands answers," November 22, 2010, available online at: https://tinyurl.com/bdmdsn6f. *New Zealand Herald* video, November 21, 2010, available on Facebook: https://www.facebook.com/watch/?v=176658269017025

John Key, seated on left; Peter Whittall standing, addressing the December 2, 2010, memorial event. (NZ Government House/Office of the Governor-General, CC BY 4.0., via Wikimedia Commons. Cropped.)

with Prime Minister John Key and the governor-general. He declared, "While we mourn our lost mates, we are still working continuously to bring them home." As we wrote at the time on the WSWS, the fact that Whittall was given this platform to pose as a great "mate" to all his workers, while his company was officially under investigation from police and the DoL, proved that the government's real priority was protecting the company.

It also underscored that the royal commission, announced by Key just a few days earlier, had nothing to do with holding anyone accountable. Indeed, its chair Judge Graham Panckhurst later declared at the start of the inquiry: "No one is on trial, there are no sides, no one will win or lose."

On December 1, 2010, we wrote on the WSWS: "Its purpose is not to establish the truth about the conditions that led up to the disaster. On the contrary, as government spokesmen, including Energy Minister Gerry Brownlee have intimated, it is to put on a show of 'learning the lessons' so that the way can be cleared for the industry to 'move on'—allowing the unrelenting pursuit of profits to resume."

This proved absolutely correct. The royal commission documented many of the flagrant safety breaches at Pike River, but it had no power to compel testimony from Whittall and others, who refused to answer questions that would incriminate them.[9]

It recommended some cosmetic changes to health and safety laws that have done nothing to address the real cause of workplace deaths. In 2019 there were 108 workplace deaths—the worst toll in nearly a decade. That was the year of the Whakaari/White Island eruption—an avoidable tragedy, which claimed 22 lives, caused by the utter negligence of tourism companies which made immense profits from taking visitors to this extremely dangerous active volcanic crater.[10]

The DoL, police and judicial system protected Whittall and others. In 2013, Pike River Coal was found guilty of safety breaches and ordered to pay $3.41 million in reparations, but the company was bankrupt and refused to pay. In 2012, VLI Drilling, a subsidiary of Valley Longwall International, which was contracted for drilling work, pleaded guilty to three charges of unsafe practices, and was fined the negligible sum of $46,800. Three VLI employees—Josh Ufer, Ben Rockhouse and Joseph Dunbar—perished in the disaster.

VLI's workers had been drilling in high-methane areas of the mine but VLI made no regular safety checks of its equipment. On the day of the first explosion, the drill rig's methane gas sensor was checked for the first time in five months and found to be faulty. The DoL noted that "the accuracy of the gas sensor and the protection it was intended to provide could not be relied on."[11]

Joseph Dunbar, aged 17, was the youngest victim of the disaster, and died on his first day underground. His father Dean told the WSWS: "He just wanted to pay his own bills and start his career. He trusted the people that took him underground, he trusted the people that managed the mine. He knew nothing about anything."

---

9. See Appendix E for the WSWS's response to the royal commission in November 2012.
10. In March 2022, Inflite Charters pleaded guilty to charges relating to the eruption and was fined $227,500. Twelve other organisations and individuals will face trial in 2023.
11. "Drilling company fined negligible sum for safety breaches in New Zealand mine disaster" https://www.wsws.org/en/articles/2012/11/pike-n03.html

Joseph Dunbar as a young boy (Photo by Dean Dunbar); *Joseph's photo from his Pike River ID tag* (Source: Royal Commission on the Pike River Coal Mine Tragedy).

Twelve charges were laid against Whittall, the only individual to be charged, for breaches of health and safety. These were dropped by WorkSafe (the rebranded DoL) in a backroom agreement in 2013 with Whittall's lawyer, in exchange for a one-off, unsolicited payment to the families from PRC. Despite the overwhelming evidence against Whittall and the company, Ministry of Business, Innovation and Employment (MBIE) spokesman Geoffrey Podger stated that the prosecution was dropped because "the public interest was not met by continuing with a long costly trial with a low probability of success."[12]

In December 2013, the MBIE and Whittall's lawyers denied that the payment had been agreed in return for charges being dropped. Judge Jane Farish described the payment as a "side issue" in the decision not to prosecute. She told the families: "Some of you will ... believe that this is Mr Whittall buying his way out of a prosecution. I can tell you that it's not."

Prime Minister Key said there had been no deal made to drop the charges. At the same time, he defended MBIE's decision, saying PRC's payment to families was "the best we can do" and preferable to the government spending "millions and millions" on prosecuting Whittall.[13]

Several family members denounced the deal as a travesty of justice and

---

12. "'Not appropriate' to continue Pike boss prosecution," *Stuff*, Dec.12, 2013.
13. "Key: Whittall case could have been costly, heartbreaking," *NZ Herald*, Dec. 16, 2013.

sought a judicial review. The Supreme Court finally ruled in November 2017 that the decision to drop charges was unlawful, but the charges were never reinstated. No one from WorkSafe, MBIE or the National government has faced any consequences for perverting the course of justice.[14]

Labour and its allies move to contain anger

For many years, the Pike River families continued to wage an extremely significant campaign for truth and justice. Following the 2011 election, the National Party government reneged on its initial promise to re-enter the mine and recover the bodies.

In 2016, the state-owned company Solid Energy (which had bought the mine from Pike River Coal's receivers) attempted to seal the mine. Work on the seal was only stopped after families and supporters blockaded the road to the mine in November, gaining widespread support from workers, farmers, and small business owners. Allied Concrete announced on November 23 that it was withdrawing from a supply contract with Solid Energy out of respect for the families.

Anna Osborne, whose husband Milton died in the mine, told the WSWS in December: "We have tried for six years now to get some sort of closure. The families who took action were sick of remaining dignified and quiet and going along with what the government said. We thought this was a huge injustice for our guys and we needed to do something about it. If we allow them to put concrete over the entrance that would be permanently entombing our men."

She continued: "We do not just want to bring our loved ones out. We've had no proof as to why this happened. This could provide the evidence we need. It could point the finger at a lot of people that didn't do their job proper-

---

14. See Appendix F for the WSWS's report on the October 2017 Supreme Court hearing.

ly. The government don't have the will and they don't want to go in there."[15]

The EPMU, which merged with other unions to form the E tū union in 2015, took no part in the 2016 protest. The union had hundreds of members employed by Solid Energy but refused to mobilise them to stop the company's attempt to seal the mine. This year, E tū endorsed the Labour government's decision to end the underground investigation and seal the mine.[16]

With the 2017 election approaching, however, the Labour Party and its allies, NZ First and the Greens, sprang into action, seeking to contain the anger over Pike River and exploit it for votes. All three parties declared they would re-enter and investigate the mine.

On November 20, 2016, for example, Little wrote: "The Government claims it's not safe to enter the drift and try to get any bodies in there out. That's not true. Experts, both local and international, say the mine is now stable. We can get those men out, and secure evidence regarding the cause of the explosion. It can be done."[17] On Facebook on November 19, Little stated: "John Key promised the Pike River families he would get the bodies out. I believe that, when you make a promise, you've got to keep it. It's safe to enter the mine now but National's moving to seal it forever. I'm standing with the families. They deserve justice."

Some family members have raised that NZ First put pressure on Labour to promise to re-enter Pike River. It would be a dangerous mistake to have any illusions in this right-wing party. NZ First was founded as a breakaway from the National Party in 1993. Before that, its leader Winston Peters was part of the government that launched the sweeping deregulation of the mining industry. In the Ardern government, Peters was deputy Prime Minister. His main priority was not Pike River but spending billions of dollars on the military and

---

15. "Families of disaster victims blockade road to Pike River mine" https://www.wsws.org/en/articles/2016/12/23/bloc-d23.html
16. See Appendix A.
17. "Andrew Little: Promises to Pike families must be kept," *The Standard* blog, Nov. 20, 2016.

strengthening the alliance with the United States.

After the election, Ardern and Little promised that the new Pike River Recovery Agency (PRRA) would work closely with the families to see that justice was done. On November 20, 2017, Little said in a Facebook video: "We now have a dedicated project to see if we can get into the mine and recover the remains of any of those men, but also to find out what actually happened, so we might better understand the cause of this tragedy. What I'm really going to be making a big point of is: the families will be involved every step of the way."

The PRRA's website says that it is "working in partnership with the Pike River families." This is false. In fact, the government is now disregarding the wishes of the majority of the families by refusing to even contemplate a further exploration of the mine workings beyond the roof-fall, where there is likely to be crucial evidence.

Minister Little confirmed on March 23, 2021, the decision he had fore-shadowed in a Cabinet paper one year earlier: there would be no more funding to continue the underground investigation into the causes of the disaster. Little flatly rejected the advice of international mining experts that the mine workings could be safely entered (this is discussed in more detail in the next article).

The government's decision to renege on the election promises, and its pretence that these promises were never made, has come as a shock to many. But it did not surprise the WSWS. We wrote on January 6, 2018:

"The Labour-Greens-NZ First coalition government... is posturing as a friend of the Pike River families. It is undoubtedly concerned that continuing protests over the disaster could become a focal point for broader working-class opposition to poverty wages, dangerous working conditions, and a regulatory and judicial system rigged in favour of big business and the rich... The WSWS warns that the government's pledges cannot be trusted." We noted that the appointment of former EPMU leader Little as the minister in charge of Pike River, and former NZ Army chief Dave Gawn as the PRRA chief executive, showed that the re-entry project "will be guided, above all, by the needs of big business and the political elite."

We completely reject the Ardern government's claim that there isn't enough money to properly investigate the 29 deaths. Under the pretext of the pandemic, tens of billions of dollars have been found to bail out mostly large businesses, including Fletcher Building, Air New Zealand, SkyCity, which have sacked thousands of workers. Billions more are being printed by the Reserve Bank to buy up bonds from the commercial banks. Hundreds of millions are now being spent to renovate parliament. There is limitless money for the banks and big business, and nothing to secure the basic rights of working people who have died in a preventable disaster.

The Ardern government has used different tactics to try and achieve what the National Party was unable to do: to shut down the investigation and make sure that no one faces any serious charges. The Pike River families were able to mount a determined struggle against the National Party government by maintaining their political independence from every party in parliament and from the unions. They ran a democratic committee where all the families could have a say. Labour calculated that it needed to divide the families and stop them from appealing directly for support from other workers. As part of the PRRA, the government attached the Family Reference Group (FRG), which it said would represent the majority of the 29 families. The FRG is an unelected body which only has three family members (Anna Osborne, Sonya Rockhouse and Rowdy Durbridge) and two advisors: Rob Egan, a consultant who has advised Labour Party leaders, and Tony Sutorius, a documentary film maker close to the unions.

Most of the families were kept out of important decision-making. The FRG issued a statement on March 30, 2021, saying: "Families accept, with heartbreak, Andrew Little's advice that there will be no more government money to expand the project at this time." Several family members objected that they had not been consulted.

Cloe Nieper, whose husband Kane died in the mine, told Radio NZ: "I didn't agree to [the FRG statement], so I don't know why they're saying that we all agreed to it... I feel like I've been blindsided." Bernie Monk, Dean Dunbar, Carol and Steve Rose made similar comments. Altogether, 23 of the 29 families indicated that they did not agree with the FRG statement, and that they wanted a feasibility study conducted to explore the mine workings.[18]

For new workers' organisations and a socialist party

These experiences contain critically important political lessons about the role of the Labour Party and the trade unions. The ruling class is increasingly relying on the unions to suppress the class struggle. In the United States, Democratic President Joe Biden and the leading Republican Marco Rubio have both campaigned in favour of unionisation at Amazon. They are not doing this to advance workers' interests. Rather, these big business politicians are terrified by the prospect of a rank-and-file movement of workers emerging outside their control.

The same tendency can be seen in New Zealand, where the Ardern government is relying on the unions to block workers' resistance to its brutal wage freeze policy announced this month. The New Zealand Nurses Organisation and the teacher unions pushed through sell-out agreements in 2018 and 2019, which basically froze wages and failed to address the staffing crisis in hospitals and schools. They will again be called upon to suppress the immense anger

---

18. The families opposing the government's decision later dropped to 22; they were represented by the Pike River Families Group Committee. Minister Little eventually admitted that the FRG did not genuinely represent the Pike River families. A statement released on September 14, 2021, said: "Towards the tail-end of 2019 the Minister foreshadowed to the Family Reference Group that going beyond the drift was unlikely. The Minister now accepts that the families who were not represented by the Family Reference Group were not advised and were not included in this communication...

"[The Minister] accepts that his decision not to explore the feasibility of re-entering the mine workings should have been communicated to all Pike River Family members before it was presented to Cabinet. The Minister accepts this caused hurt to several family members as a result of this." This grudging admission, completely buried by the media, was made in exchange for an agreement by the Pike River families to withdraw their application for a judicial review of the decision to seal the mine.

brewing up among their own members—just as Pike River Coal relied on the EPMU to suppress opposition to the conditions in its mine.

What is the way forward? There is undoubtedly widespread anger and disillusionment about the unions. In 1985 nearly half of all workers were in a union. Ten years later, it was down to 20 percent and today the figure is below that. In the private sector, just 7 percent of workers are union members. For decades, strikes practically disappeared. Social inequality has soared as corporations ratcheted up the exploitation of workers in a one-sided class war.

In opposition to the union bureaucracy, our movement, the International Committee of the Fourth International (ICFI), ahead of our annual online May Day rally, called for the building of an International Workers Alliance of Rank-and-File Committees (IWA-RFC). We explained that this initiative "will work to develop the framework for new forms of independent, democratic and militant rank-and-file organisations of workers in factories, schools and workplaces on an international scale. The working class is ready to fight. But it is shackled by reactionary bureaucratic organisations that suppress every expression of resistance."

The IWA-RFC "will be a means through which workers throughout the world can share information and organise a united struggle to demand protection for workers, the shutdown of unsafe facilities and nonessential production, and other emergency measures that are necessary to stop the spread of the virus."

We advanced this call "within the framework of the perspective of world socialist revolution." The formation of new workers organisations is not "a substitute for the building of the revolutionary party. Action is required, but serious action must be based on program and principles. Sustaining and developing a network of independent organisations requires the development of a socialist leadership in the working class."[19]

---

19. "Forward to the International Workers Alliance of Rank-and-File Committees!" https://www.wsws.org/en/articles/2021/04/24/pers-a24.html

The Pike River deaths and the subsequent cover-up demonstrate the urgent need for a genuine socialist party. This is the only way to combat the enormous political pressure that is brought to bear by the ruling class to disarm and divide workers, through the instruments of the Labour Party and the unions, and all their allies.

The disaster has also exposed several pseudo-left organisations that hover around Labour, the Greens and the union bureaucracy and falsely call themselves socialist. These include the International Socialist Organisation (ISO) and Organise Aotearoa. The ISO last wrote about Pike River in November 2012, in an article that presented the EPMU as a vehicle for defending workers and said nothing about its role in paving the way for the disaster.[20] On the ninth anniversary of the disaster, in 2019, Organise Aotearoa posted on Facebook a statement by the Council of Trade Unions also promoting the unions as a means to ensure workplace safety. A third outfit, Socialist Aotearoa, which has links with the Unite union, has not published a single statement on Pike River.

These are not socialists, but groups representing the interests of the upper middle class. Instead of fighting to unify workers and expose Labour and the unions, they defend these organisations, while obsessively promoting divisive identity politics, based on race, gender and sexuality.

The ICFI fights to unify workers internationally against capitalism and all the groups and parties which pretend that the system can be reformed. We have described the pandemic as a "trigger event" in world history that has intensified and exposed all the contradictions inherent in capitalist society.

To defend policies that are leading to mass death and record social inequality, politicians around the world are promoting authoritarian and outright fascist forces. And to counter its economic decline, the United States is now

---

20. The ISO praised the EPMU for its call, following the disaster, for the reintroduction of worker-elected check inspectors (https://iso.org.nz/2012/11/06/the-tragedy-at-pike-river-an-indictment-of-capitalism/).

threatening war against China and Russia—which would be a nuclear war that would threaten the very existence of human civilization.

Because New Zealand has experienced only 26 deaths from the pandemic, it is portrayed internationally as an exception, a progressive country with a "kind" and compassionate prime minister. This is a fraud. Pike River and the CTV building collapse show that New Zealand is not immune from the brutality of capitalism, which is pushing workers and young people to the left.

We are in a period of history, like the First World War and the Great Depression, where the future of humanity will be decided in revolutionary struggles, involving masses of people.

The First World War was only ended by the intervention of the masses of workers and peasants in the Russian Revolution, led by the Bolshevik Party, which sparked revolutionary uprisings throughout Europe. Today too, the immense crisis facing the world cannot be resolved outside of a revolution.

That is why workers and young people must make serious political decisions. There is more than enough wealth in the world, if it was not hoarded by a tiny number of billionaires, to end inequality and to organise society along rational, scientific lines, to put an end to nation states and therefore to put an end to war, and to address climate change.

I urge everyone listening to this meeting to study our perspective, read our articles and make the decision to join the Socialist Equality Group and fight to build a section of the International Committee of the Fourth International in New Zealand. Thank you for your attention.

Families of Pike River mine disaster victims applied for a judicial review of the government's decision to seal the mine, at the High Court in Wellington, June 4, 2021: (Left to right) Carol Rose, Steve Rose, writer Fiona Kidman, Kalani Nieper, Bernie Monk, Cloe Nieper, lawyer Paddy Brand, Kath Monk. (Photo by WSWS Media)

What is the government trying to bury in Pike River mine?

First published June 17, 2021. Expanded for this publication.

The Labour Party government's plan to abandon the underground investigation into the 2010 Pike River coal mine disaster has sparked significant opposition. Over 6,000 people have signed a petition supporting 22 of the families of the 29 miners who died in the mine, urging Prime Minister Jacinda Ardern to reverse the decision.

The government wants to pull investigators out of the mine after exploring only the drift or entry tunnel. It is refusing to re-enter the mine workings, including the site of the underground fan that may have ignited the first explosion on November 19, 2010. More than a decade later, no bodies have been recovered and no one has been prosecuted for the disaster, despite a 2012 royal commission finding that Pike River Coal Ltd. breached numerous safety laws and regulations and turned the mine into a death trap, in order to cut costs.

The families' petition on Change.org states: "We're just two piles of coal from answers. Two piles of coal from finding out what really caused the Pike River tragedy... If they seal the mine now they will lock that critical evidence away forever, with it, any chance of finding out what happened, of holding those responsible to account, and of making sure it never happens again. We must not let them do it."

One of hundreds of people who commented on the petition, Kylee, wrote: "A family member's body is in that mine. How can you simply think not returning them home is okay? Disgraceful to say the least, what if it was your family member?" David said: "The Government cannot be allowed to continue with this cover up. They are wasting millions elsewhere (America's Cup [yacht race] for example) but cannot spare 8 million dollars to get to the truth."[21]

The *World Socialist Web Site* has published dozens of letters demonstrating international support for the families, and outrage at the lack of justice for the men who were killed at work. Expressing sentiments shared by many, Tracey stated: "Everyone deserves the right to know what happened in the mine and [to] hold people accountable. This was no accident and could happen again." Others denounced Minister Andrew Little's statement last month that the government has to prioritise "the living." Rachel wrote: "This is really about protecting big business. Protecting the working class of New Zealand does not appear to be a priority. Neither is compassion or closure for all the victims of the Pike River disaster, either living or deceased."

The 22 families, organised as the Pike River Families Group (PRFG), are supporting an application for a judicial review, filed with the Wellington High Court on June 4 by Bernie Monk, to try and stop the government from permanently sealing the mine with concrete before the criminal investigation is completed. International mining experts, who previously advised the government's

---

21. The petition, titled "Help stop critical evidence in Pike River Mine from being locked away for ever!" had gained more than 6,600 signatures by April 2022.

Pike River Recovery Agency (PRRA), are supporting the PRFG and have outlined how the two roof-falls ("piles of coal") can be safely passed using standard mining practices.

The Ardern government would be incapable of enforcing this agenda of cover-up without the assistance of all sections of the political elite in NZ, including the Greens and the unions. The corporate media has barely reported on the PRFG's struggle and supports the push to seal the mine without anyone being prosecuted.

On March 26, Newstalk ZB's right-wing host Mike Hosking, who has long opposed the Pike River families' fight for justice and defended chief executive Peter Whittall, praised Andrew Little as "my political hero of the week" for refusing to provide more funding for the investigation. More recently, on June 8, the *Otago Daily Times* editorialised that the families should "move on," that the re-entry operation had become too "expensive," and "there must be limits." The various pseudo-left organisations that support the unions have written nothing since the Ardern government came to office in 2017.

The government is relying on the trade union bureaucracy, which has maintained a conspiracy of silence about the cover-up of one of the country's worst industrial disasters. The Engineering, Printing and Manufacturing Union (EPMU, now called E tū) had 71 members at Pike River when it exploded; E tū's current national secretary Bill Newson told the WSWS on May 5 that the union "supports the government's position regarding not re-entering the main mine."

Minister for Pike River Re-entry Andrew Little, who ordered the shutdown of the investigation, was the head of the EPMU when Pike River exploded. This is a clear conflict of interest since the union was complicit in the disaster. It took no action to stop workers entering the mine and kept quiet about the unsafe conditions underground. In the days after the disaster, Little defended the company's safety record.

The government's move to seal and walk away from the mine as quickly as possible raises disturbing questions of vital importance to the working class in

New Zealand and internationally: What is the government seeking to bury, and why?

Little says it is too technically difficult, unsafe, and expensive to proceed into the mine workings. These claims are demonstrably false. The real aim of the government, representing the NZ ruling class, is to cover up the causes of the disaster to protect those responsible for the 29 deaths, including: Pike River Coal and its backers; the Labour Party and National Party governments who dismantled safety regulations; and the Department of Labour (DoL) and union bureaucracy, which knew the mine was unsafe and did nothing to protect the workers.

The importance of the underground evidence

The royal commission of inquiry's 2012 report is a damning indictment of Pike River Coal and the regulators who allowed the mine to operate. It stated that the company "had not completed the systems and infrastructure necessary to safely produce coal," with methane ventilation and drainage systems that were completely inadequate, and "the drive for coal production before the mine was ready created the circumstances within which the tragedy occurred."

There were "numerous warnings of a potential catastrophe at Pike River," the report said, including "reports made by the underground deputies and workers. For months they had reported incidents of excess methane (and many other health and safety problems). In the last 48 days before the explosion there were 21 reports of methane levels reaching explosive volumes, and 27 reports of lesser, but potentially dangerous, volumes. The reports of excess methane continued up to the very morning of the tragedy. The warnings were not heeded."[22]

The commission highlighted the lack of a second egress, or emergency exit—a clear violation of the law. The company designated the ventilation shaft,

---

22. *Royal Commission on the Pike River Coal Mine Tragedy*, Vol. 1, p12.

with a 105-metre ladder, as the second egress, but the royal commission found that it would have been "difficult, perhaps impossible" to climb in the event of an emergency, and "after the explosion the vent shaft became a chimney for flame and noxious gases."[23]

It found that the DoL, which knew about the lack of a second egress and other safety problems, "should have prohibited Pike from operating the mine until its health and safety systems were adequate."[24]

Royal commissioner Stewart Bell, Queensland's former head of mine safety, told Radio NZ in September 2014 that he was surprised no one had been prosecuted over the many blatant breaches he had helped to document. Twelve charges against Whittall for breaches of health and safety laws had been dropped the previous year, in a back-room deal with Whittall's lawyers. The royal commission's terms of reference, set by the National Party government, prevented it from recommending charges.

On July 17, 2013, police announced they were concluding their initial criminal investigation of the disaster. In a statement police acknowledged the "ample evidence that there were widespread departures from accepted standards of mine operations," but insisted that they could not lay manslaughter charges without physical evidence showing a "causative link to the specific events which led to the explosion."

Without such evidence from inside the mine, the royal commission could not reach a firm conclusion about what sparked the November 19 methane gas explosion. It identified possible sources including diesel engines, "contraband" items taken into the mine, "frictional ignition" from mining activities, "sparks from the non-flameproofed underground fan," or another electrical fault.[25] The commission highlighted the extreme negligence of Pike River Coal's decision to place its main fan underground. Coal mines never do this, largely be-

---

23. *Royal Commission*, Vol. 2, Part 1, p226.
24. *Royal Commission*, Vol. 1, p12.
25. *Royal Commission*, Vol. 2, Part 1, p190.

cause "a malfunction of the fan or its motor can be a source of ignition."[26]

Installing main fans underground in coal mines is expressly outlawed in some countries, including the United States and Canada, and the International Labor Organization's code of practice assumes that they are installed on the surface. Establishing that the fan played a role in the Pike River disaster would reinforce the immense danger of such practices.

The Independent Technical Advisory Group (ITAG), supporting the Pike River Families Group, released a Conceptual Development Plan in early May for the recovery of the main fan site, beyond the two coal-falls. ITAG is led by former chief inspector of mines Tony Forster and includes coal methane expert Dr David Creedy and mines rescue expert Brian Robinson.

The ITAG document, drawing on the findings of the royal commission and subsequent investigations, pointed out that "commissioning problems [were] reported at the main fan in October 2010, associated with overheating fan control cabinets, sparking at the main fan drive shaft and subsequent re-moval of a brass sealing ring from the main fan shaft bulkhead wall. The latter created a potential air leakage path which could have allowed methane enriched return air (in the 5% - 15% explosive range) to flow over non-explosion proof electrical equipment including the fan motor and associated control switches."

The ITAG noted that "part of the main fan electrical power supply cabi-net, LC601, and associated plastic circuit board pieces" were blown out of the ventilation shaft by the force of the explosion. This "important evidence" was "photographed and retrieved from the mountainside to the Pike River manag-er's office," but it then "disappeared." If it had been forensically tested, the de-bris could have indicated whether the fan sparked the explosion.[27]

The disappearance of this physical evidence was only made public in Feb-ruary 2019. Minister Little told Radio NZ that he thought the police and

---

26. ibid., p84.
27. Pike River Independent Technical Advisory Group, "Conceptual Development Plan for Main Fan Access Roadway Recovery," p4. Available here: https://tinyurl.com/mwjf6bsf

WorkSafe would have the fan cabinet component "stored somewhere [with] all of the exhibits and the material they collected." But the item has never reappeared, and police have never explained what happened to it. Police admitted to destroying other exhibits, including a scientific report and items of clothing, earplugs and breathing apparatus that may have belonged to some of those who died underground.[28]

It is not clear whether the royal commission knew of the existence of the main fan debris. Tens of thousands of documents, photos, videos, and other evidence examined by the inquiry in 2011–2012 have been embargoed for 100 years. The Department of Internal Affairs told an academic researcher in 2017 that the embargo was necessary "to protect personal privacy as well as to maintain implied and existing undertakings in relation to confidentiality"—a statement which explains nothing (whose privacy and what undertakings?).[29]

This extraordinary decision prevented any independent analysis of the evidence presented to the commission. Bernie Monk and Dean Dunbar, whose sons Michael and Joseph died at Pike River, have demanded that the embargo be lifted and accused the state agencies of a cover-up.

Other evidence inside the mine may have been literally covered up with concrete in late 2011, when the mine was controlled by Pike River Coal's receivers, and Steve Ellis, who was the manager when the disaster happened, was still employed as the statutory mine manager. Essentially, police allowed the crime scene to be controlled by some of the same people that were supposedly the subjects of a criminal investigation.

Electrical engineer Richard Healey, who has worked with some of the Pike families for the past two years to investigate the disaster, revealed in 2020 that he had obtained leaked documents and video footage, showing that hun-

28. "Crucial evidence from New Zealand mine disaster missing" https://www.wsws.org/en/articles/2019/03/13/pike-m13.html ; "New Zealand police destroyed Pike River mine disaster evidence" https://www.wsws.org/en/articles/2019/09/13/pike-s13.html
29. Felicity Lamm, "Pike River Mine: Bring them home," *Briefing Papers*, May 1, 2017. https://briefingpapers.co.nz/pike-river-mine-bring-them-home/

dreds of cubic metres of concrete were poured into the mine down a narrow ventilation shaft. The concrete, he said, flooded the so-called "fresh air base," an area that included emergency equipment and where any survivors of the first explosion might have congregated.[30]

The suppression, mishandling and destruction of evidence makes it even more imperative that there is a full underground investigation of the mine, conducted by independent forensic and mining experts.

Is it safe to enter the mine workings?

The previous National Party government initially promised to re-enter Pike River mine and retrieve all the remains of the 29 men. On September 22, 2011, Prime Minister John Key told a meeting of the families: "I'm here to give you absolute reassurance we're committed to getting the boys out, and nothing's going to change that. So, when people try and tell you we're not... they're playing with your emotions."

This promise was ditched after National was re-elected in the November 2011 election. Government ministers would later claim, falsely, that the mine had been a raging inferno, with human remains and evidence destroyed by explosions and fires, and that the mine was not safe to re-enter.

In fact, images taken deep within the mine, by cameras lowered down bore holes in 2011, showed that much of the mine workings were relatively undamaged. Items, including a wooden pallet and a plastic bucket, were recorded on video, as well as at least two apparent bodies. Some of the footage was made public in June 2017 after it was leaked to the families.

In the lead-up to the 2017 election, after families protested against the National government's plan to seal the mine, the opposition Labour Party, the Greens and the right-wing NZ First Party all promised to re-enter the mine to

---

30. "Tonnes of concrete poured into 'critically important' Pike River Mine air feed where miners could have gathered - Electrical expert," *Newshub*, November 21, 2020.

search for evidence and bodies. In 2019, the Labour-led coalition government began the re-entry of the 2.3 kilometre drift. This was done safely by the PRRA, with assistance from some of the same mining experts who are now pushing for the exploration of the mine workings.

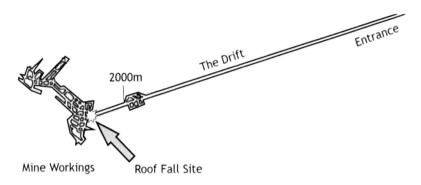

Mine Workings   Roof Fall Site

The cynicism of the government's rejection of the ITAG plan is underscored by the fact that, when Labour was in opposition, it heaped praise on the same experts. In parliament on December 13, 2016, then-Labour leader Andrew Little asked then-Prime Minister Bill English: "When he says it should be up to the experts to determine whether re-entering the mine is safe, is he aware a report saying re-entry is safe has been written by Dr David Creedy, vice-chair of the UN Group of Experts on Coal Mine Methane, and Bob Stevenson, former UK principal mines inspector, and that the report has been peer reviewed and endorsed by the United Kingdom's leading mines rescue expert, Brian Robinson, and by mining ventilation experts John Rowland and Dr Roy Moreby?"

Little also asked: "Why does [English] not do the right thing, listen to the families, and fulfil his government's promise to do everything he can to get their men out?"

Bernie Monk told the WSWS: "Now that [Forster's] actually got a plan together to finish this job, they're showing him no respect. It's upsetting to see how they've treated all the experts."

The ITAG's Conceptual Plan responds to Minister Little's claims in the media that the area around the roof falls is "inherently unstable." This position was echoed by the E tū union's Newson, in his statement to the WSWS: "The rockfall blocking off the main mine is substantial and we have been advised that overcoming that obstacle is a considerably more complex and dangerous challenge under mining regulations."[31]

The ITAG plan states that, based on analysis and observations by the PRRA and previous studies, "there is no information to suggest that stability either above or below ground, at or around the roof fall zone... has measurably altered since 2010 as a result of the explosion or fire."[32]

The experts outline a proposal "using standard mining practices by which recovery of the main fall and access to the underground ventilation fan could be safely achieved." They explain how the coal-falls can be excavated and workers can systematically advance, installing "steel-arch lined access tunnel supports"—a common method used in mines internationally.[33]

In its official response to the ITAG plan to proceed past the two roof-falls and into the main fan area, the PRRA does not dispute these points. There is no mention of "inherent instability." The agency admits that the experts' plan is "technically feasible," and safety issues can be mitigated.

In rejecting the Conceptual Plan in late May, Little did not mention safety concerns. He referred to the "significant costs associated with the Plan," "unquantifiable technical issues," and the fact that Cabinet had given the PRRA no "mandate" to explore the mine beyond the drift.[34]

In a June 4 statement responding to Little, the Pike River Families Group Committee objected to the justice system being "subjected to arbitrary fiscal restraints in this way." It added that the PRRA's claim that entering the mine workings would cost upwards of $20 million "cannot be substantiated and ap-

---

31. See Appendix A for Newson's statement.
32. "Conceptual Development Plan," p13.
33. ibid., p22, p18.
34. Pike River Recovery Agency, "Briefing of the initial high level review of the 'Conceptual Development Plan for Main Fan Access Roadway Recovery,'" May 26, 2021, p3.

pear[s] to be guesswork." Little has refused to authorise a proper cost assessment; the ITAG estimated that its plan would cost $8 million.

As family members have pointed out, this pales in comparison to hundreds of millions of dollars wasted by the government on yacht races and the renovation of parliament. Billions have also been spent over the past year to bail out corporations and shield the rich from the economic crisis triggered by the COVID-19 pandemic.

The PRRA claimed that the ITAG plan "takes no account" of work being undertaken by police to drill boreholes into the mine workings, including one that will allow "visual examination of the site containing the fan housing and the motor room beside it." The agency continued: "Police believes... [this] will substantially corroborate or discount the various theories presented to the Royal Commission of Inquiry as to the cause of the initial explosion" and bring the investigation "to a point where charging decisions can be made."[35]

There is no reason to accept these assurances—particularly given the police decision in 2013 not to lay charges because of the lack of physical evidence. Pike River family members have described the new plan as "second-best" evidence-gathering, which is less likely to stand up in court.

Aside from costs, the PRRA gave no reasons why the drilling of boreholes should preclude a manned examination of the fan site. Nor has the government explained why this work justifies the mine being permanently sealed. If a camera lowered down a borehole discovers a body, or other significant physical evidence, a permanent seal will ensure that it can never be physically recovered and forensically examined.

Were there survivors after the November 19 explosion?

The re-entry of the mine workings could shed light on whether any of the 29 men survived the first explosion on November 19. In the days that followed the

---

35. ibid., p7.

explosion, Pike River chief executive Whittall and the police told the public and the families that a rescue operation was being discussed, based on the assumption that there could be survivors trapped underground. When a second explosion occurred on November 24, the authorities declared that there was no longer any chance of survivors.

The royal commission's report stated that Mines Rescue could not have mounted a rescue attempt because of "a lack of information" about the mine's atmosphere, due to inadequate gas monitoring systems. The damaged underground ventilation unit and lack of a second egress added to the dangers facing rescuers.

The report criticised decision-making at the mine site, saying: "Instead of decisions being made at Pike River, where mining and rescue experts were gathered, many were made by non-experts in Wellington. This slowed the emergency response and could have impeded a rescue had one proved possible."[36] Police were in charge and in continual discussions with Pike River Coal, Mines Rescue and DoL officials, and there were conflicting views on whether the mine should be immediately entered or sealed to prevent further explosions.

The royal commission concluded that the men "probably died instantly, or from the effects of noxious gases and oxygen depletion soon after the explosion on 19 November." However, the report noted that images taken by a laser scanner lowered into the mine's "fresh air base" on November 24, just before the second explosion, showed that a box containing self-rescue breathing apparatus was open. It said "how the lid was opened remains unexplained," but that it might have been opened by a survivor.[37]

Other information supports the possibility of survivors. Miner Allan Dixon's family said they received a phone message from him minutes after the first explosion. His sister-in-law Leona told the *Australian* on November 23, 2010: "It was something very brief, like 'I love you.'" Pike River Coal and the

---

36. Royal Commission, Vol. 1, p26.
37. Royal Commission, Vol 2. Part 1, p231.

police insisted it was not possible for any call to be made from within the mine.

Mines Rescue general manager Trevor Watts told the royal commission in September 2011 that no one could have survived because a compressed air line into the mine was ruptured.[38] However, an expert report commissioned by the DoL, dated January 2012, estimated that the pipe had ruptured 2,300 metres into the mine, i.e. possibly beyond the roof-fall.[39] Electrical engineer Richard Healey told the *Press* on July 24, 2020 that the pipe could have provided breathable air for any trapped workers, who he believed could have survived even the second explosion. He said the compressed air was switched off two hours after the second explosion, when police announced that there was no longer any possibility of survivors.

A thorough underground investigation could also help establish what sparked the second explosion, which was not looked at in detail by the royal commission. Healey has suggested, based on analysis of electrical data and documents leaked to the families, that the blast happened when a conveyor belt going into the mine was switched on. *Stuff* reported on September 26, 2018: "Documents show police did discuss using the conveyor belt prior to the explosion to help any survivors escape the mine." Police admitted that this was discussed but denied turning on the belt.

Serious questions remain about what happened between the first and second explosions, including the decisions made by police and Pike River Coal.

Who is the government protecting?

Following the release of the ITAG's Conceptual Plan, Minister Little told *Newshub* on May 12 "we've reached the end" and "we have delivered justice for the families." This statement is patently false. Prior to the 2017 election, Labour and its allies led the families, and the public, to believe they would serious-

---

38. "Pike mine 'should have been sealed'", *Stuff*, September 21, 2011.
39. Energy NZ on behalf of the Department of Labour, "Pike River Coal Audit Report for November 19, 2010," January 2012, p10.

ly consider entering the mine workings after recovering the drift.

For more than a decade, successive National and Labour Party governments, along with the police and the judicial and regulatory system, have prevented anyone being prosecuted for actions that led to the deaths of 29 people. This demonstrates the reality of class justice under capitalism: rich businessmen are protected.

By burying the evidence, literally and figuratively, the Ardern government is continuing a cover-up to ensure no one is held accountable. This includes Pike River chief executive Peter Whittall, his predecessor Gordon Ward and managers Steve Ellis, Doug White and Robb Ridl. The company's board of directors included chairman John Dow, Ray Meyer, Tony Radford, Stuart Nattrass, Arun Jagatramka and Dipak Agarwalla. Pike River Coal was about 31 percent owned by New Zealand Oil & Gas (NZOG). Two Indian-based companies, Gujarat NRE Coke and Saurashtra Fuels, owned 10 percent and 8.5 percent respectively.

These individuals have never given a full, public account of their actions at Pike River. They were not required to speak at the 2012 royal commission, and those who did appear, including Whittall and Ellis, could choose not to answer specific questions.

They continued to hold high-paying positions. Ellis went on to work as operations vice-president for Compliance Coal's underground mine in Canada. Whittall moved to Australia, where he is the chief executive of a retirement home. Ward became the owner and manager of a supermarket, also in Australia. Radford continued as a director of NZOG until October 2013. Dow was a director of Glass Earth Gold, a gold exploration company, until 2014.

While the government falsely claims that it cannot pay for a thorough investigation of Pike River, none of these wealthy individuals or companies have been made to contribute anything. Following the disaster NZOG and the Bank of New Zealand (Pike's creditor) shared in an insurance pay-out of more than $70 million.

Those responsible for the environment that led to Pike River include successive governments, led by Labour and National, which dismantled the state's specialist mines inspectorate during the 1990s and allowed mining companies to self-regulate. Governments ignored warnings from mining experts that the deregulation would inevitably lead to disaster.

The unions covering the mining industry did not organise workers to oppose these attacks, which were aimed at slashing costs and increasing profits. Like their counterparts internationally, the NZ unions responded to the globalisation of production by enforcing ruthless pro-corporate restructuring from the 1980s onwards. These upper middle-class organisations collaborated with businesses and the state to impose mass redundancies, including about 4,000 job cuts in the state-run mines.[40]

In justifying the abandonment of the underground crime scene, Little provocatively told *Newshub* on May 12: "When you're in government, you've got to weigh up competing priorities. For me, my priority now is the living."

In response, Healey wrote on Facebook: "Like Little, my priorities are with the living. In the last decade 60 to 70 people every year go to work and come home in a box... the living are important, we owe it to them to make sure that the guilty are held to account for their actions at Pike—because if we don't, we will surely see the tragedy at Pike happen again."

Kath Monk, whose son Michael died in the mine, told the WSWS: "Little was the national secretary of the EPMU back in 2010. Well, he should have been as concerned about the living back then, because some of the men underground were members of that union."

Steve Rose, whose stepson Stuart Mudge died in Pike River, asked: "What could be so awful in that mine that they don't want brought into the light of day?... Andrew Little knows stuff, and the stuff that he knows, they obviously consider to be damaging to the government."

---

40. Marcia Russell, *Revolution: New Zealand from Fortress to Free Market*, 1996, p119. After Pike River, the unions assisted in imposing hundreds more layoffs at Solid Energy's mines. The state-owned company was finally liquidated in 2018 after its assets were sold off.

Union officials knew that Pike River mine had no second egress, that workers had protested over the lack of emergency equipment, and that there had been methane gas ignitions in the mine in 2008.[41] But the EPMU never publicly criticised Pike River, let alone organised industrial action to stop its life-threatening operations. After the explosion, EPMU leader Little initially defended the company's safety record.

As minister responsible for Pike River in the Labour government, Little is continuing his role as a defender of big business by ending the investigation. He is also preventing further scrutiny of the EPMU's role. Any genuine investigation would have to examine the union's records and correspondence, which would reveal the extent of its collaboration with Pike River's management, and how much the EPMU bureaucrats knew about conditions in the mine.

With the stampede to end the underground investigation, the government is sending a clear message that corporations can get away scot free with criminal practises that lead to mass deaths. This cannot be allowed to happen!

The working class must support the Pike River Families Group's fight for a thorough, independent and transparent investigation of the disaster, and for the prosecution of those responsible. **Stop the cover-up! Stop sealing the mine! End the embargo on the royal commission's evidence, and stop protecting corporate criminals!**

41. Rebecca Macfie, *Tragedy at Pike River Mine*, Awa Press, 2013, p180.

Bernie Monk and Steve Rose protesting in July 2021. (Photo by Carol Rose)

Father of Pike River victim: "Ten years on, we still haven't got justice"

This is a slightly edited speech by Bernie Monk, whose son Michael died in the disaster. The speech was recorded and played in the SEG's May 8 webinar.

There has been a huge coverup at Pike River. I could sense it from very early on. The real turning point in this story was when someone came to me just before Easter 2011 and showed me a photo of self-rescue boxes open underground [suggesting that men could have survived the initial explosion]. We then went to the police and we got them to show us the evidence for this.

As we went on and interviewed people we realised how bad it was. It's just been an endless story. To think that we're 10 years down the track, still haven't got justice, still haven't got accountability, and the families had to go out and do an investigation of their own. Because there's the same police force overseeing the present investigation of the disaster that did the initial investigation. I just don't think that's right.

I think it's wrong that the families have had to do their own investigation and had to protest outside the mine to stop it from being sealed in late 2016. ACC,[42] who were shareholders in Pike River Coal, and the Bank of New Zealand, which was a major creditor, have never come and knocked on our door and said that they want to help to retrieve the men.

The National Party government continuously lied to us, claiming it would re-enter the mine to investigate and retrieve the bodies. Now we've nearly come full circle. The official investigation has come to the end of the drift tunnel, and now we've got to fight the Labour Party government to finish the job.

We've got a good band of experts, top people from overseas, and I'm humbled by the faith that they've had in the families and by all the work that they've done. They have done this investigation and explained on paper how to do this job.

I've asked Andrew Little: Who are his experts? I've written to him three times. I've had no replies. I asked him, when he spoke about the amount it would cost to finish the job: Who are the people who are investigating the cost of re-entering the mine workings? Still, I've had no answer. I've rung local Labour Party MP Damien O'Connor—still no reply.

But our fight is going to continue. We're going to bring the truth out, and we've got all the information now to be able to do that.

I have to take my hat off to people that have come and helped us. The biggest turning point was the select committee hearing in 2017 that was arranged by writer Dame Fiona Kidman, and Tony Forster. Along with myself and other family members, we went up to Wellington and spoke at a select committee. NZ First leader Winston Peters put the stake in the ground and said that he would go down into the mine. He knew that this job could be done.

New Zealand, and the world: you've got to realise that we've seen images of bodies taken by cameras lowered into the mine. We've got SCADA [electri-

---

42. The Accident Compensation Corporation (ACC), NZ's state-owned accident insurance provider, owned $20.5 million in shares in Pike River Coal at the time of the disaster.

cal] data from the mine. We've got all the information. Yet the police do not want to share anything with us. They say that sharing information with the families could undermine their investigation. Well, they've had 10 years to investigate this. We've had 18 months, and we've found out that some information given to the royal commission by the Department of Labour and police was incorrect.

How is the official investigation being conducted? They're trying to wear us out, they're trying to sweep this under the table and hoping that we'll go away. Well, it's not going to happen.

The people I hold responsible, and that should be in the courts, are not only Pike River. There is also the Department of Labour (now called WorkSafe): they knew that this mine was unsafe; Mines Rescue: they said in the royal commission that this mine had never had a second form of egress; and the EPMU: union members went to them and said that this mine was unsafe. What did they do? They did absolutely nothing.

Now the government claims the investigation will cost too much money. Well, if they are going to renovate the parliament buildings for over $200 million, they can spend a bit more money on getting justice and accountability. What I'm saying to New Zealand is: do not let corporate manslaughter be governed by money. That's what happened here. Pike River Coal paid money out, and they let people off the charges that should have laid in the first place. That's what our fight's all about.

Kath Monk, Michael's mother, added:
I want people to realise that another reason the families are so insistent on having someone accountable for what's happened, is so that everyone in New Zealand who goes to work can be sure that they come home safely. Our men didn't. No one's been held accountable for that, and that's not right.

"Stop the sealing of that mine and let us get the answers!"

This statement was posted on Facebook by Olivia Monk, Michael's sister, on May 17, and reposted on the WSWS on May 24, 2021. The post was shared hundreds of times, reflecting growing support for the Pike River families' fight for truth.

My brother Michael was 23 years old when he was killed at work. He was a qualified carpenter who was working for a company that went into receivership, and needed a job. That's when he started working at Pike River. As a builder, rather than a miner, he didn't have the knowledge that many others did underground, he relied on the miners, the managers, the board that ran the company to keep him safe. Little did he know that he was working in an absolute death trap that could've blown at any time, and there were many who knew this and still put the men to work every day.

Unfortunately, on Friday the 19th of November 2010 at 3.44pm, Pike River blew, and it killed my little brother, and 28 others. Our lives from that moment have been changed forever.

For 10.5 years we have been fighting hard to find out the truth of what happened that day. We have a fairly good idea, but only because we have fought behind the scenes to bring the truth to light. It's taken so many experts who have given their time for free over the years, and sometimes it's just taken luck, people giving us evidence they don't realise is important, and even sometimes it's been stuff that has been leaked by people that know of the injustices.

The police, several governments, politicians, Pike River Management have been so fixated on getting that mine sealed and locking away any evidence that would bring a conviction. They have even gone so far as to lock away all the evidence from the Royal Commission for 100 years, so that no one now will be alive when the embargo is lifted, a move that has never been done before. And why is that?

Michael, Olivia and Alan Monk (Photo from Olivia Monk's Facebook post)

We have produced a feasibility study that proves that going a tiny bit further to the fan inside the mine won't cost anywhere near what they are saying it will, and will hold the answers. Yet in 19 days' time, the Recovery Agency is set to seal that mine.

Minister Little stated the other day that he was more interested in focusing on the living, after years of using us as a political pawn to get himself and his party elected. Now I don't disagree that there are the living that need this money too. However, we found billions left over from COVID funds a couple of weeks ago, we managed to spend $12k on a funeral of a turtle, millions on a boat, so in the grand scheme of things, this figure isn't big bickies for a government.

And let's just talk about the living, my brother WOULD BE LIVING if he hadn't been killed by greedy selfish people that knew what they were doing was wrong. Some people call that murder.

And further on the living, why are we still sending living people to work in New Zealand and around 100 of them each year don't come home?

NO ONE has been held accountable for 29 men's deaths, NO ONE has taken responsibility, NO ONE has learnt anything from this, and NO ONE has any consequence if this happens again, we just keep killing people at work. Now that to ME, seems to be a way we can be focussing on the living.

I know a lot of you are tired of hearing all about this. I'm tired of living it every day, but I don't get to escape it. Every day I think about the different scenarios of how Michael may have died. The fact that we have seen images of bodies slumped over sitting against the rib of the mine and self-rescuer caches open make it very possible that Michael was alive for hours or days, waiting to be rescued, and no one came. It's a pretty hard pill to swallow, and something I think about daily. There are a lot of people very keen to stamp out these theories, but the fact is that there is evidence, and could be more if we are able to get into the mine. Why are these people keen to stamp out all the evidence, what have they got to hide, and who are they trying to protect?

I would love to know the truth of what happened on that day, and the days after during the rescue and recovery. I would love to see people held to account for the murder of 29 men.

I would love to be able to fall asleep every night knowing the answers to all my questions so I could have a decent sleep.

I would love to see accountability shown and the lives of 29 brave men honoured.

Stop the sealing of that mine, and let us get the answers!

Writer Fiona Kidman supports demand for continued investigation of Pike River
May 28, 2021

Writer Fiona Kidman has played an important role in supporting the fight for the re-entry of Pike River, and truth and justice for the victims. Kidman, whose many novels include *This Mortal Boy*, which won the top award for fiction in the 2019 New Zealand Book Awards, told the WSWS, "In my writing over many years I think I've tried to demonstrate some social conscience... I think if we start to neglect injustice to any part of society, then we're failing."[43]

In late 2016, Kidman and her husband Ian joined the picket organised by the Pike River victims' families on the road to the mine site, aimed at stopping the National Party government's attempt to seal the mine, entombing the bodies and evidence inside.

Ian, who died in 2017, had worked on the West Coast "as a schoolteacher for a couple of years, and he had a very strong feeling for the Coast," Kidman said. "One evening we were just watching the picket line when the sealing of the mine was happening and we said to each other: 'They look a bit lonely, do you think we should go and help them?' When we got there, it was very obvious to us that what was happening was not right."

In early 2017, Kidman promoted a petition initiated by her friend Alexandra Dumitrescu, calling on the government to re-enter the mine. Kidman joined Tony Forster, a former chief inspector of mines, Bernie Monk, Sonya Rockhouse, whose son Ben died in the disaster, and Anna Osborne, whose husband died, in presenting the petition and accompanying statements to a parliamentary select committee hearing in February 2017.

At the time, the National government and Solid Energy made unsubstan-

---

43. Kidman's essay "At Pike River," reflecting on the disaster and the families' fight against sealing the mine, was published in March 2022 in her book *So Far, For Now* (Penguin Random House).

tiated claims that it was too dangerous to re-enter and explore even the drift. Forster and other experts presented evidence that demolished these claims.

Now, with the Labour government intent on shutting down the manned re-entry of Pike River, Forster, as well as David Creedy and other international mining experts, are supporting the majority of the families' push to continue the investigation and re-enter the mine workings.

Kidman described the present situation as "ironic, really and truly. It is the same scenario playing out under a Labour government." She noted that in her submission to the parliamentary committee, she had said: "at the time of the disaster, John Key said that no effort or money would be spared to bring the bodies of the deceased out of the mine."

"Well, of course they didn't do anything," Kidman said. Later, when Labour came into office, "one of its promises was that they would right this wrong of Pike River. When they are so close to getting through that drift, and when there is a plan to continue, why stop now? I simply do not understand it."

She continued: "I'm not pointing fingers at any particular person or people, because I don't think that there is a lot to be gained by that. As far as Andrew Little is concerned, I would prefer to think that I would be supporting him and a Labour government to keep going."

Kidman questioned claims made by the Pike River Recovery Agency that it would cost upwards of $60 million to explore past the coal-fall. "I don't know where this huge sum came from," she said, adding that Forster and the other experts have estimated the operation will need only another $8 million. "Tony has been proven right over and over again. So, listen to him now."

"We spend millions and millions of dollars on overseas war graves and on recovering and repatriating people from overseas," Kidman added. "Why are we not trying to repatriate these human remains? It is still important. People say to me: 'Let them be, they're entombed and it's a beautiful place.' It's not a beautiful place, it's the wreckage of a mining disaster."

Kidman was frustrated that public attention to the Pike River families seemed to have been worn down because of "this huge delay in doing what should have been done years and years ago... A lot of people in the cities have tuned out. It gets up my nose, because they say, 'It's been a long time and it's over now.' But it's not over." She said people's attitudes would be different if Wellington's Mount Victoria tunnel had collapsed with people inside.

"I do understand that there's a division in the ranks of the families, and the government seems to be listening to one side and not the other. I don't understand why that is," Kidman said. (Six of the 29 families are not challenging the government's decision.)

"If you look at someone like Bernie Monk, in 2011 he was being hailed as potentially the New Zealander of the Year. He received honours for supporting that community. He's still the same person. Bernie is Bernie. They're not different people, they're still honourable, gutsy, down-to-earth people who are trying to tell the truth as they see it."

Kidman thanked the *World Socialist Web Site* for its articles supporting the Pike River families, saying: "I think they're very good and very hard-hitting. You're certainly prepared to lay yourselves on the line... Somebody has to say these things, so good for you."

The families' and supporters' picket, July 9, 2021. (Photo supplied by Kath Monk)

Families picket road to prevent the sealing of Pike River mine

July 9, 2021

This morning, family members of some of the 29 workers killed at Pike River, as well as their supporters, held a protest blocking the road to the mine site. The action is part of the fight by 22 of the 29 families to stop the Labour Party-Greens government from permanently sealing the mine and preventing the forensic examination of evidence and human remains.

In late 2016 and early 2017, several families gained widespread support when they blockaded the same road, preventing the then-National government from sealing the mine with concrete. With the 2017 election approaching, Labour and its allies, the Greens and NZ First, feigned support for the families. Now, however, Labour, supported by every other party and the trade unions, is seeking to shut down the investigation.

Bernie Monk told *Stuff* the families aimed to stop the Pike River Recovery Agency's work, which began this week, to install two seals in the mine. He appealed to the workers involved to "down their tools [and] support us."

"We are prepared to stay here until they sit around the table and come to some agreement and don't seal the mine until they finish the investigation," Monk said.

About 30 people joined this morning's picket. The families are calling for more supporters to join when they resume next week.

Olivia Monk wrote on Facebook: "If we let the mine be sealed permanently, we destroy any evidence to find out the cause of the explosions at Pike, and anyone being held accountable. All the evidence from the Royal Commission has already been locked away for 100 years. It is important to all workers of New Zealand, and mine workers around the world. Everyone should have the right to come home safe from work." The post has received more than 100 likes and dozens of shares.

Despite the media reporting as little as possible on the families' fight for truth and justice, they have growing support from ordinary people, as seen in an online petition signed by 6,310 people, and hundreds of social media comments.

Carol Rose, whose son Stuart died in the mine, told the WSWS, "it's a shame that it's come to this. We have tried really hard, as a group, to engage the government in a conversation and they choose not to engage. We decided we needed to exercise our democratic right and protest."

She said the government was trying to "bulldoze" and "bully" the families. The families have applied for a judicial review of the government's decision, "so, in good faith, they should be stopping work until there's a resolution reached" in the courts. Instead, in recent weeks the PRRA has worked more rapidly than ever before to withdraw equipment and prepare the mine to be sealed.

Dean Dunbar said the protest's "objective was to send a message to the workers that the families don't agree with what you're doing, and you guys need to make a decision. If they drop tools, I think it will have an impact like no other." He said it was "absolutely cruel" that the government had left the families with no other options.

The families have made clear to the PRRA and the police that they are not seeking to prevent the ongoing work of drilling boreholes into the mine, which is part of the police investigation. "But as for their retreating from the drift," Dunbar said, "we will be stopping the workers doing that, sealing that mine and entombing our children."

Ben Joynson, who was 10 when his father William died in Pike River, hoped the protest would gain support "because this is just a low blow to the families if they seal it after everyone fighting to keep the investigation going." Continuing the search for evidence was "the most honourable thing to do for the men who worked in those conditions" and their families and "the right thing to do morally," he said.

Cloe Nieper, who lost her husband Kane, hoped that the protest would demonstrate that most families opposed the decision to seal the mine, and generate "more public interest in what's actually going on, because the media haven't been covering things." She told the WSWS prior to the protest, "I've read some of the comments [on the families' petition] and they're pretty amazing. I think people are very supportive and a lot of people still want to know what we want to know, they want answers and they want us to have justice."

Minister Little has made no public statement on the families' protest. Nor has the E tū union, which supports the government's actions. The disaster and its aftermath show how the unions have been thoroughly integrated into the structures of corporate management and the state.

The WSWS calls for working people, in New Zealand and internationally, to support the demand for a thorough underground investigation to determine precisely what caused the disaster, and for an end to all plans to seal the mine. We urge readers to share this article, send us statements of support and, where possible, join the families' protest.

An urgent warning: Government moves to seal the mine
July 23, 2021

The Pike River Recovery Agency (PRRA) resumed work this week on installing the first of two seals in the Pike River underground coal mine. On July 14, several days after the families' protests began, the PRRA said it would cease work on installing what is described as a temporary seal 170 metres within the drift.

However, an email sent to the families on July 19 from PRRA chief executive Dave Gawn stated: "As of this morning the workforce were at the mine site to continue the mandated tasks including work on the 170m rated seal." He made clear that the work was only paused for a few days, in response to the protest, and that "the Agency's intent and the Government mandate has not changed and work will continue to seal the mine."

The PRRA did not publicly announce that this work had resumed. It is clearly nervous about the widespread support that the families have received.

After completing the 170-metre seal, the agency will begin work on a permanent, concrete seal 30 metres inside the tunnel. Gawn said it "will not be in any position to contemplate work on the permanent seal for another 4 to 6 weeks yet."

The government could well speed up this work, given its clear determination to seal the mine. There is no reason to believe that any notice will be given before work starts on the final seal. In 2016, when the National Party government and Solid Energy first attempted to seal the mine, the families said they had been misled to believe the seal would be a temporary barrier.

The National government was forced to back down by protests by the families and supporters. Now, Ardern's Labour Party-led government is seeking to finish what National was unable to do.

"I think it's pretty clear there's no will or desire to get to the evidence required to secure convictions," Dean Dunbar told the WSWS. The PRRA, he said, "has one motivation and only one, and that is to seal that mine as quickly as possible." He added that it was not possible to trust the PRRA's statements about the time frame, asking, "When has anything to do with Pike River been upfront and honest?"

Dunbar noted that the PRRA was seeking to pile on the costs that would be involved in continuing the underground investigation. It has stripped technical equipment from the mine, claiming it would cost $4.2 million and take three months to reinstall.

The government has repeatedly made clear its intention to seal the mine, even before a court has ruled on the families' application for a judicial review of this decision. Dunbar said, "When a government needs to do something to protect its own, they will make sure that the gloves are off and they will achieve it by any means they can, and they will think about the consequences later. There will be none anyway."

He pointed out that when the Pike River royal commission released its findings in 2012 there were expressions of shock, throughout the world, at how the company had broken several laws and ignored multiple warnings that the mine could explode. "Yet nobody is in jail, no one's been charged, no one's been held accountable."

Labour and National, and their allies the Greens, NZ First, the ACT Party and the Māori Party, represent the interests of big business. The record shows that these parties are determined to protect those responsible for the 29 avoidable deaths at Pike River. The government is relying on crucial assistance from the trade union bureaucracy, which supports the plan to seal the mine.

The WSWS warns that there can be no confidence that any ministers or party leaders will be swayed by appeals. The only way to stop the mine from being sealed is through the intervention of the working class. We call on working people to support the demands for an immediate end to the sealing of the mine, and for a full underground investigation.

Former Deputy Prime Minister says New Zealand government is covering up mine disaster

August 4, 2021

The ruling elite is extremely nervous about the widespread support from working people, in New Zealand and internationally, for the majority of the 29 families, who are demanding an end to the sealing of the mine, and a full underground investigation.

The media is attempting to keep the population in the dark, reporting as little as possible. On Friday July 30, *Newshub* reported that "work to seal the mine has ceased temporarily." In fact, work was only delayed due to bad weather and a protest on Thursday on the road to the mine.

On July 30, Winston Peters, leader of the right-wing nationalist New Zealand First Party, visited Greymouth to pose as a supporter of the families. Peters served as deputy prime minister and foreign minister in the Labour-led 2017-2020 government, which also included the Green Party. NZ First lost all its seats in parliament in the October 2020 election, getting only 2.6 percent of the votes.

Peters held discussions with some of the family members, as well as technical experts including former chief inspector of mines Tony Forster. Peters told *Newshub* the government was reneging on the 2017 coalition deal between Labour and NZ First. He said: "I know what a cover-up looks like, and this thing stinks to high heaven."

All three parties promised in 2017 to re-enter the mine to look for human remains and gather the evidence needed to prosecute those responsible for the disaster. Minister for Pike River Re-entry Andrew Little announced in late March 2021, however, that the government was ending the underground investigation, having only explored the drift.

The Ardern government is certainly engaged in a cover-up, aimed at protecting the company bosses and those who enabled their extremely dangerous operations. The *World Socialist Web Site* warns, however, that no confidence can be placed in NZ First. Peters is using the Pike River issue in a cynical attempt to resurrect his political career. When NZ First was in government, it went along with the efforts to shut down the investigation.

The Labour-NZ First-Greens coalition government indicated that it would stop the Pike River re-entry well before the October 2020 election. In an official Cabinet paper dated March 9, 2020, Little stated: "I do not intend to bring any proposal to Cabinet to move beyond the roof fall at the end of the drift and explore the main mine workings." On June 10, 2020, Little again told a parliamentary committee: "I'm very clear, and Cabinet has been very clear, there are no additional resources" to go beyond the drift.

There is no record of Peters or NZ First's other Cabinet minister, Defence Minister Ron Mark, raising any objections to these statements. On October 7, shortly before the election, Peters was asked by the *New Zealand Herald* if he still supported the Pike River re-entry. Peters replied that he did, and wanted justice for the families, but he did not mention his own government's refusal to enter the mine workings. Peters was clearly hoping to return to government in coalition with Labour, in which case there is every reason to believe he would have continued to support sealing the mine.

In the first term of the Ardern government, NZ First and Labour worked together closely on policies to slash immigration, ramp up military spending and strengthen ties with the United States. The government also transferred tens of billions of dollars to the rich in the form of low taxes, bailouts, and subsidies, while starving essential services including the healthcare and education systems, which provoked nationwide strikes by teachers, nurses, doctors, and other healthcare workers. The decision to shut down the Pike River investigation and shield the corporate criminals from accountability is of a piece with these broader pro-business policies and attacks on the working class.

NZ First has been part of successive governments which created the deregulated, pro-business environment that led to the Pike River disaster. Prior to the founding of NZ First in 1993, Peters was a senior MP in the National Party government that launched the wholesale destruction of mine safety regulations. Legislation passed in 1992 disestablished the specialist Coal Mines Inspectorate and abolished the requirement for worker-elected safety check inspectors.

NZ First entered a coalition government with National from 1996–1998. As treasurer and deputy prime minister, Peters told a business audience on February 11, 1997 that he supported a "deregulated, competitive and open market," with reduced costs for businesses, including the "lowest possible taxes."[44]

In 1997, the government's Crown Minerals unit granted New Zealand Oil & Gas, Pike River's major shareholder, a licence to develop the mine. Former chief inspector of mines Harry Bell told the royal commission in 2011 that Crown Minerals received no support from mining experts to understand mine plans, which was "always a recipe for disaster." He said, "Pike's plans should... never have been approved," and would not have been under the old legislation.

NZ First again played a major role in Helen Clark's Labour Party-led coalition government from 2005–2008, with Peters serving as Foreign Minister. During this time, Pike River Coal began developing its mine. In 2007, the company told the Department of Labour it planned to install its main ventilation unit underground, despite the known risks. The agency didn't object, and there was nothing in the legislation to prevent the company from doing so. By this point the mining industry was completely deregulated. According to the 2012 royal commission report, "from 2001 to October 2011 the number of mining inspectors fluctuated between one and two," covering the whole country.

The record shows that no capitalist party can be relied on to stop the sealing of Pike River mine. The government's push to bury the truth will protect those responsible for the disaster and pave the way for more flagrant workplace safety violations and deaths. Only the intervention of the working class can stop this cover-up.

---

44. Peters' speech can be read at: https://thedailyblog.co.nz/2016/09/07/expose-winston-peters-the-1997-speeches-and-neo-liberal-tendencies/

Government lies about mine re-entry promises
August 12, 2021

Newshub incorrectly reported on August 7 that "a permanent seal won't go on until the police investigation is over." The first of two seals has already been completed 170 metres inside the mine and preparations are underway for a second seal to be installed at 30 metres.

Speaking to *Newshub*'s "Nation" program, Minister for Pike River Re-entry Andrew Little sought to justify the shutdown of the investigation with a series of brazen lies. He declared that prior to the 2017 election the Labour Party only promised "to recover the drift," and this was the mandate given to the PRRA by Cabinet, which included Labour and leading members of its coalition partners NZ First and the Green Party. "That is very clear in the [Cabinet] papers," Little said.

Little accused NZ First leader and former deputy PM Winston Peters of trying to "rewrite the Cabinet minutes" by claiming that the government had led families to believe they would consider going further into the mine.

In fact, Little and the Labour Party repeatedly promised, in 2014, 2016 and 2017, to do everything possible to recover bodies and evidence from the mine, and to make all decisions relating to the re-entry "in partnership" with the families of the 29 victims.

A November 2017 Cabinet paper established that the PRRA left open the possibility of exploring the mine workings. It said: "At a point when the process of recovering the drift is well advanced, the responsible Minister will report to Cabinet on whether any further work, to assess the feasibility of re-entering the mine workings, should be undertaken."

In March 2020, however, when only a quarter of the drift had been explored, the Cabinet ruled out any additional funding. Little told *Newshub* that the government had decided the investigation into one of New Zealand's worst industrial disasters was becoming too expensive, even though there was no feasibility study conducted about the cost of entering the mine workings.

Interviewer Simon Shepherd asked: "If money wasn't an object, would you keep going?" Little replied: "The critical factor was safety." He said "experts," whom he didn't identify, had said that getting through a roof-fall and into the mine workings "was all-but impossible" without spending "hundreds of millions of dollars."

Bernie Monk told the WSWS that the Minister's statements were "absolute rubbish." He said the government had "used" the Pike River families "to get into power, and now they're just casting us aside. If he's not using money, then he's trying to use health and safety. We've proved him wrong. It's not a health and safety issue, we've gone 2.3km down the drift, we haven't had any trouble with health and safety up to now... He's continuously lying to the public on this. It's unforgivable."

In 2017, he said, "we had a Labour Party who said we're going to do everything possible to go into the mine, we're going to get your men out, we're going to get accountability for you... Now they're saying no, we didn't say that."

Monk pointed out that internationally respected mining experts had produced a Concept Plan on behalf of the families showing that the mine workings could be safely re-entered for less than $8 million.

Little himself praised the work of these experts when they advocated for drift re-entry in 2016. In the *Newshub* interview, however, he dismissed their report, and falsely claimed that no expert had "put their name to" it. In fact, David Creedy, Brian Robinson and Tony Forster have all spoken out publicly in support of their findings.

Little rejected the Concept Plan in May, not because of safety concerns, as he now claims, but due to the "significant costs" involved, which the PRRA estimated would be over $20 million—not "hundreds of millions."

The government would not be able to seal the mine and lock away the evidence without the assistance of the trade union bureaucracy. Media commentator Neale Jones, a former official for the EPMU and advisor to Little, told *Newshub* he had "sympathy" for the families but insisted that Little had "fulfilled the promise he made." In 2012, when he was the EPMU's communications director, Jones lashed out at the WSWS on Facebook, accusing it of "misinformation" for highlighting the fact that the union had not publicly criticised Pike River's unsafe conditions in the lead-up to the disaster, or taken action to shut down the mine.[45]

The union, now called E tū, is continuing its role as an adjunct of the business elite by endorsing the government's actions. "Where have they been?" asked Monk. He said the message being sent to businesses was: "Come and invest in New Zealand: You can kill people in the workplace and get away with it and walk away, it's not going to cost you a razoo."

In an earlier interview with the WSWS, Monk noted that he had approached a union official at a memorial service for Pike River families in 2019 to ask them to push for an investigation of the mine workings. "He said to me: 'Bernie, you know they're never going through that rockfall.'" Monk replied: "You want us to come up here every year and put our fists in the air and say 'solidarity' when there's 11 of your men sitting buried in Pike River and you haven't got off your arses."

Monk praised 30,000 New Zealand nurses and healthcare workers for "standing up to" Little, who is also the Minister of Health, by carrying out a nationwide strike on June 9 after rejecting a sell-out pay agreement presented by the union. Outside parliament, Little was shouted down by a crowd of thousands of health workers when he tried to defend the government's record.

The government claims there is not enough money to adequately fund public hospitals—just as it says there is no money to properly investigate 29 workplace deaths at Pike River. The same government, like others around the world, has given tens of billions of dollars to businesses, to protect them from the economic crisis triggered by the pandemic.

The working class is coming into ever-more direct struggle against the

---

45. We responded to Jones' outburst at the time. See: "A reply to a New Zealand union official," August 20, 2012, https://www.wsws.org/en/articles/2012/08/nzpr-a20.html

government's austerity measures, which are being enforced by the unions. A major issue for healthcare workers is the lack of workplace safety due to under-staffing, which could lead to disaster if an outbreak of COVID-19 occurs. The WSWS calls on these workers, and the working class more generally, to support the Pike River families' fight for the full truth about what caused the 2010 disaster, and for those responsible to be brought to account for their criminal practices.

Nurses and healthcare workers gathered outside parliament during the June 9, 2021 strike. Health Minister Andrew Little spoke for about one minute, feigning sympathy for the workers, before he was drowned out by boos and angry shouts. A key issue in the strike was unsafe conditions caused by under-staffing in hospitals. (Photo by WSWS Media)

Public anger over cover-up of Pike River disaster

September 29, 2021

The corporate media continues to black out the broad opposition in the working class to the government's actions.

Malcolm Campbell, whose son, also named Malcolm, died at Pike River, responded in the Facebook group Uncensored Pike to the September 18 WSWS article reporting on the sealing of the mine:

"Now we have come to the end of our fight for justice and recovery of our loved ones killed doing their jobs for these incompetent so-called mine managers and corrupt government." He asked how the dangerous mine got approved and was allowed to operate.

"So sad for all the families it has come down to our loved ones [remaining in this] hellhole, they deserved better," Campbell said. "We as a family thank all our family and friends here and around the world for their everlasting support and kind words over these difficult years, so sorry we couldn't get Malky home, thinking of you all xx."

In the Facebook group Underground Miners, which includes thousands of mineworkers from around the world, the WSWS's article received more than 200 reactions and 50 comments, almost all denouncing the NZ government.

Troy Reynolds wrote: "Very disappointing for the families and yes it feels a little like a cover up. Even if there is no fault to be had I am sure there are some poor mums and dads who will now go to their grave without closure."

Jamie Harris commented: "The government should give the families some closure over this. They want to know. They also want other companies to learn from this, so others don't have to go through it. No family should have to go through waiting for their loved ones to come home from work."

In the Uncensored Pike group, Karyn Stewart was one of hundreds of people who have commented, opposing the sealing. She questioned the role of Andrew Little, Minister for Pike River re-entry, who was leader of the EPMU when the mine exploded.

"Isn't this a conflict of interest?" Karyn asked. "How can Little front the recovery when he was a part of the union that allowed the health and safety violations?" She added: "The issues with Pike have been beset with corruption from beginning to end and one of the problems seems to be that the mainstream media are silent (have been silenced) over publishing anything."

Another commenter said the government had lied to the families to get elected, adding: "My heart goes out to all the families and the men and women fighting for their children's rights. This is an absolute betrayal to all involved. I am heartbroken for you all."

Marc Thomlinson, who worked at Pike River mine, wrote a statement on Little's Facebook page on September 23, saying that Little was aware of the company's violations in 2009:

"I remember the first time I met you, Andrew. I was a union delegate at an EPMU meeting held in Reefton, 2009. [...] You shook my hand at the conclusion of the meeting where we both shared a concern with the Pike River Mine in regards to the [inadequate] ventilation and secondary egress." In violation of the law, government regulators allowed Pike River to operate with no proper emergency exit. Thomlinson said to Little: "You looked me in the eye and affirmed to me that you were aware of the situation." He urged the minister to "bring our men home to where they belong, because it is the right thing to do."

The WSWS also received a statement supporting the Pike River families from Professor Maan Alkaisi, whose wife, Dr Maysoon Abbas, was one of 115 people who died in the collapse of the CTV building in the February 2011 Christchurch earthquake.

In late 2017 Brendan Horsley, then deputy solicitor-general, advised police not to lay any charges against those responsible for the building's design, despite evidence that it violated numerous laws and regulations and was essentially a death trap.

"After more than ten years the victims of the CTV building collapse are still waiting for accountability and justice," Alkaisi said. "We have been let down by the very people who are supposed to protect us and apply the rules of law. The similarities of the CTV case with Pike River tragedy [show] that our legal system is dysfunctional when it comes to ensuring justice for victims.

"This is demonstrated by the delay in starting the investigation, by ignoring significant evidence, relying on irrelevant matters, the decision not to prosecute anyone for the loss of lives, the silence of government and legal officials, the lack of accountability when it comes to influential, well-connected wealthy culprits, and not answering our legitimate questions."

He believed Crown Law, the state's solicitors, "avoid going through cases of national or even international significance" because they are part of an "old boys' club" and are "incompetent and scared" of facing lawyers hired by the wealthy.

On February 23, 2021, the day after the tenth anniversary of the Christchurch earthquake, Prime Minister Jacinda Ardern said in parliament that New Zealand would continue to "stand with" the victims.

However, Alkaisi said that the day before, "when I asked our PM to meet to explain to her in private our concerns regarding the decision not to prosecute, and victims' mistreatment, she refused to meet with me. How do you expect us to trust the politicians? How do you expect us to trust the decision Crown Law made not to prosecute was the right decision? Why were decisions made behind closed doors and without documentation? Why not conduct a just trial in front of a Judge and Jury?

"Our government has both a legal and moral responsibility to uphold our justice system to ensure it protects all citizens, and to ensure in situations where lives were lost, that those responsible will be held accountable in accordance with the rule of law. That is justice.

"The CTV collapse and Pike River tragedies will only end, when those responsible are held to account, when there is proper closure for victims and when justice is done."

Recovery 29 whitewashes the government's cover-up

November 2, 2021

The documentary *Recovery 29*, directed by Sofia Wenborn, was aired on Prime Television in New Zealand on October 26 and added to the Sky Go streaming website. The state-funded film is a whitewash of the government's decision to continue the cover-up of the Pike River mine disaster.

The film provides a superficial account of the Pike River Recovery Agency's (PRRA) work since it was established following the 2017 election. Wenborn's 2016 documentary *Pike River* addressed some of the conditions in the mine leading up to the explosion. The new film focuses on how the PRRA made the mine's drift tunnel safe to re-enter, by venting methane gas and using nitrogen gas to neutralise the atmosphere, before entering to retrieve debris and equipment for forensic examination.

Many of the victims' families had hoped that the Ardern government would uncover the full truth about the disaster. *Recovery 29*'s narrator Bryan Crump declares that the PRRA was set up to "right the wrongs" and "recover the 29."

The film does not point to the glaring conflict of interest in the fact that the Minister for Pike River Re-entry is Andrew Little, who, as leader of the Engineering, Printing and Manufacturing Union (EPMU) at the time of the explosion, defended the company's safety record.

The Labour government, with Little playing a key role, pulled the plug on the underground investigation before it had the chance to uncover human remains and the most significant evidence in the workings. Over the past month, the PRRA has been installing a permanent, 30-metre-thick concrete seal at the portal of the mine—a decision opposed by 22 of the 29 victims' families.

Recovery 29 sets out to justify these actions. Crump states: "Pushing on is not an option... to go beyond the roof-fall would require a whole new plan."

Some workers at the PRRA express frustration at being told the job will be abandoned. Shane McGeady, who had friends among the Pike River 29, says not going beyond the roof-fall "frustrates the shit out of you, knowing you're so close." Another worker comments that "it's like doing a half-finished-job."

Rowdy Durbridge, whose son Dan Herk died in the mine, and who is among the minority of family members supporting the government's decision, says the re-entry "didn't achieve what I really wanted, and that was to get [the bodies] out." However, he echoes Minister Little's position that too much has been spent on the re-entry already, and it would be too expensive to proceed into the mine workings. Durbridge is a member of the Family Reference Group, part of the PRRA, which does not represent most of the families.

PRRA chief operating officer Dinghy Pattinson acknowledges that the decision will be seen "as a lost opportunity." But he defends the government, saying it never promised to go beyond the drift, and that "there is no more money" to go further.

The film does not question these statements. There is no mention of the detailed proposal by the Independent Technical Advisory Group (ITAG), showing how the mine workings could be safely re-entered.

Recovery 29 devotes just over five minutes to the protests and legal action supported by 22 of the Pike River families, against sealing the mine. Bernie Monk points out in the film that Minister Little broke his promise that the government would make a proper assessment of whether to explore beyond the mine workings once the drift had been recovered.

Monk says in the film: "I feel sorry for [the PRRA workers]. They've got to walk down the street and see us and think: 'I sealed Michael Monk into the mine.'"

Monk told the WSWS the film was "very light-hearted" and "weak." Much of what he raised in his interview was edited out; including questions about whether the miners survived the first explosion on November 19, only to die following a second explosion five days later. He noted that police were not investigating the cause of the second explosion.

Monk pointed out that the film makes no mention of the widespread support for the families on the West Coast and more broadly.

The film concludes with the end-title: "The families settled their legal dispute with the government outside of court," without giving any further explanation. Carol Rose, whose son Stuart died in the mine, told the WSWS this made it sound like the families had been paid. In fact, the legal action was withdrawn in exchange for an admission from Minister Little that the Family Reference Group did not represent many of the families, and that the government had not properly consulted the families on its "decision not to explore the feasibility of re-entering the mine workings."

Pattinson says in *Recovery 29* he hopes there will be prosecutions resulting from the evidence gathered from the drift tunnel, "because you can't have 29 people dying in a workplace and no one being held accountable." Police are currently drilling boreholes and lowering cameras into parts of the mine workings; it is unclear whether useful evidence can be gathered in this way, without a manned re-entry.

The film presents the police investigation uncritically. There is no mention of revelations in 2019 that crucial pieces of evidence have gone missing, including a door to a control panel on the underground fan, which was blown out of a ventilation shaft and found shortly after the mine exploded. If tested, it could have revealed whether the fan was a source of ignition.

All in all, *Recovery 29* is thinly disguised propaganda, "a big pat on the back for the government," as Carol Rose put it. It seeks to give the false impression that everything possible has been done to find out the truth about the disaster, to shore up the severely damaged credibility of the Ardern government, and to justify what is, in fact, an ongoing cover-up.

More bodies photographed after Pike River mine sealed

December 21, 2021

On December 19, New Zealand Police announced that "two sets of probable human remains and one set of possible human remains" have been seen in footage taken by a camera lowered down a borehole into Pike River coal mine. The borehole was drilled into an area of the underground mine workings known as One West Mains.

This follows a similar announcement last month that two or three bodies were found near a piece of mining equipment called the Alpine Bolt Miner (ABM), where a borehole had been drilled. Cloe Nieper told Radio NZ on November 18: "I just wish the government wasn't in such a hurry to close or to seal the mine for god only knows what reason," preventing the bodies from being recovered.

Following the November announcement, Minister Little repeated the false claim that it "simply was not safe, nor technically possible to get through the most unstable and dangerous part of the mine site," the roof-fall blocking the mine workings.

While there is immense public interest in Pike River, and widespread support for prosecutions, the latest police announcement was timed for release just a few days before Christmas. The news has also been largely overshadowed by the spread of the Delta variant of COVID-19 and the discovery of Omicron.

The bodies in the latest images have not yet been formally identified and have not been shown to the families. However, the images were taken in an area where up to five workers were thought to have been working: Jacobus Jonker, Malcolm Campbell, Ben Rockhouse, Josh Ufer and Joseph Dunbar.

Police superintendent Peter Read said that police were seeking to "do everything possible to provide the men's loved ones with as much knowledge as possible about what happened." The borehole drilling program was initially scheduled to end this year but has been extended, with another borehole to be drilled in January.

Read told a press conference that police have "a preliminary view on what's happened," but did not explain what it was. Asked whether there would be enough evidence to lay charges, he said any answer would be "speculating."

The press conference raised serious questions about the conduct of the investigation. Read was asked why it had taken 11 years to gather the images. He gave no convincing answer, saying simply that technology was now more advanced, allowing for clearer images to be taken. In fact, there was already the technology to take high-quality images underground a decade ago.

Dean Dunbar told the WSWS he was grateful that police had personally called him to inform him that his son's remains might have been found. However, he criticised the decision to delay the borehole drilling program until after the mine was sealed. He said that if superintendent Read's announcement had been made a few months ago, before the final seal, "there would have literally been thousands of people driving to stand at those gates [on the road to the mine] and demand those boys come home."

Several family members and supporters protested at the gate in July and sought to challenge the decision to seal the mine in court. They had the support of thousands of ordinary people, and of international mining experts, who argued that the mine workings could be safely entered to examine evidence and retrieve the bodies.

Dunbar said the full truth must be told about Pike River, including whether there were survivors after the first explosion, and about all the subsequent decisions made by police and government agencies.

The latest footage comes from a new borehole drilled adjacent to borehole 44, where images were taken in 2011 and concealed from the families and the public. They were leaked to the media in 2017, including images of bodies which could not be identified. According to police, the new images are much clearer.

Police have shown families some very poor images taken of the underground fan site and have not said whether they intend to conduct a more thorough examination of the machine, which may have sparked the first explosion. Dunbar said police only showed him video footage of the fan, not still photographs, which can produce much better images in dark underground conditions.

Superintendent Read refused to comment on whether any self-rescue devices could be seen in the new images. The presence of this breathing apparatus would indicate that at least some workers survived the first explosion. In November, *Newshub* reported that deployed self-rescue devices could be seen in the images taken near the ABM, according to an unnamed source.

One reporter asked Read to address families' concerns about the decision made in 2011 to pour tonnes of grout down a shaft into the "fresh air base," where survivors may have gathered after the first explosion. This would have obliterated any evidence in the area. Read replied: "I'm not going to comment on that, sorry. I don't have a great deal of knowledge on that." He said police were not investigating the issue.

Bernie Monk told the WSWS the concrete was poured into what should have been treated as a crime scene while Pike River Coal's Steve Ellis was still the statutory manager in charge of the mine. He questioned why the Department of Labour (WorkSafe) and the police had allowed this. "I've written letters to [WorkSafe] and they don't even write back to me," he said.

Monk said the families had been repeatedly lied to over the past decade. The National Party government, which wanted to prevent any investigation of the mine, falsely claimed "that everyone was ashes, that the men died straight away, there was nothing to retrieve, the mine was a burning inferno."

Electrical engineer Richard Healey wrote on Facebook in response to the latest announcement: "They covered up the [fresh air base] in hundreds of cubic metres of concrete, they sealed the evidence behind hundreds more. [Police] refuse to use the most basic of photographic techniques to image the mine properly. It's clear to me that this isn't just incompetence."

Police end borehole drilling after finding more human remains
March 11, 2022

On March 9, 2022, police announced that they had taken images of two more bodies inside the abandoned mine. A total of 6 bodies, and two possible sets of human remains, have now been sighted. After drilling 10 boreholes into the mine since June 2021, police will not drill any more, abandoning the search for the remaining bodies.

Detective Superintendent Peter Read told the media that the latest discovery was "significant," but he was "very aware that it still leaves many unanswered questions for the men's loved ones." None of the images have been publicly released.

Superintendent Read said the borehole drilling program had provided "valuable information to inform our investigation into the underground activity that led to the first explosion." He did not explain why police have decided not to try and locate all 29 bodies. Nor did he say what sort of evidence could be obtained from the images, without a forensic examination of the bodies.

According to *Stuff*, "police have drilled a borehole into the area containing the main ventilation fan." No details have been released about this. Again, it is unclear what information can be gleaned without physically inspecting the area.

Radio NZ reported that Read expects the criminal investigation will be concluded in "months, rather than years." Nigel Hampton QC, a lawyer for some of the families, said he was optimistic that there would be prosecutions. Police, however, have not said publicly whether they are considering charges against anyone.

In October 2021, *Stuff* reported that police told the families their investigation had found "gas content in the mine during October and November 2010 was high. There is evidence that management knew this and some evidence that they actively chose to ignore it. Furthermore, they either omitted or chose not to install gas monitoring devices that would have warned them of the dangers with absolute clarity."

This statement echoed the findings of the royal commission in 2012. The following year, police suspended their initial investigation into the disaster without laying charges, saying that they could not do so without retrieving physical evidence from inside the mine.

Dean Dunbar pointed out to *Newshub* that the latest discovery of bodies was in the same location where a borehole was drilled in 2011 and an image of a body was taken at the time. He questioned why it had taken more than a decade for police to revisit the area and obtain more images.

Asked by the WSWS about the likelihood of prosecutions, Dunbar noted that Pike River's chief executive Peter Whittall and the rest of the management have been under "an umbrella of protection" for more than a decade. He said they probably have evidence about what occurred in the mine that implicates government agencies.

Bernie Monk denounced the "cheque-book justice" which allowed Whittall to avoid prosecution in 2013 in exchange for an unsolicited payment to the families.

Monk told the WSWS that the discovery of bodies vindicates those families and supporters who protested last year to try and stop the mine being sealed before the investigation was concluded.

Monk and Dunbar believe some of the 29 men could have survived the first explosion on November 19. Monk said survivors could have gathered behind the roof-fall at the end of the drift, where a ruptured pipe could have been sending compressed air into the mine. The police refuse to investigate this area.

"I think the families have the right to know," Monk said. "If they don't go in and get the guys out, then at least they should put a borehole down."

Dunbar criticised police for refusing to say whether they have seen deployed self-rescue devices near any of the bodies, which would indicate that at least some of the miners survived the first explosion. "It's a simple question. If police are continuously refusing... us access to that footage, then [they should] answer the question," he said.

Monk hoped that electrical gear recovered from an area of the drift known as Pit Bottom in Stone would assist in building a case against Pike River's management. He was not sure whether this was being thoroughly examined by police.

Monk pointed to the series of false promises made to the families over the past eleven years. In 2011, then-Prime Minister John Key promised that the mine would be re-entered, but his National Party government later reneged on this. Labour made the same promise but sealed the mine without retrieving bodies.

There is widespread anger over the lack of accountability for the disaster. A typical comment on the *One News* Facebook page said: "12 years and still no remains removed from the mine, and nobody's been held accountable, can't imagine the toll this has taken on those poor families." A comment on *Newshub*'s report asked: "Why haven't the mine owners been made to recover the bodies and do the investigation or at least paid for it?" Many similar comments appeared in Facebook groups such as "Uncensored Pike" and "Supporting the Recovery of our Pike 29."

Workers should have no illusions: the experience of the last decade proves that the justice system is rigged in favour of the rich and powerful. New Zealand is far from unique in this regard. Last month, the Office of the Work Health and Safety Prosecutor in Queensland, Australia, refused to charge anyone over an underground explosion at Anglo American's Grosvenor Mine, which left five mineworkers with horrific injuries. This was despite an inquiry last year finding that the company failed to control methane gas levels and exposed workers to "unacceptable" risks.

Brother of Pike River victim denounces abandonment of underground investigation
March 19, 2022

After police announced that they had concluded their borehole drilling at Pike River, the WSWS spoke with Gordon Dixon, whose brother Allan died in the mine at the age of 59. Gordon said, "We're gutted, as a family," about the "injustice" and lack of accountability for the disaster. "Justice needs to be done, not just for us but for the rest of the country."

Gordon described the events in the 11 years following the disaster as "New Zealand's biggest cover-up." He pointed out that evidence presented to the royal commission is embargoed for 100 years. "I've got no faith in the justice system, because it depends on who you are, and if you've got money," he said.

Gordon strongly denounced the Labour Party-Greens government's refusal to allow investigators to re-enter the mine workings. "Why was the mine sealed before all the boreholes were finished?" he asked. "What if they'd found something that was really crucial? It just stays in there. This is what we can't understand, and people I talk to about it are blown away," he said. "Any other place in the world, they'd go in and retrieve their loved ones."

Experts had shown that the mine workings could be entered safely, for a cost of $7 or $8 million. Gordon said his uncle Harry Bell, who was chief inspector of mines in the 1990s, also believed it could be done. "But Andrew Little said it would cost an extra $50 million, and the coffers were empty. That's what sickened us," Gordon said.

He explained that Bell "always said if he was inspector of mines [at the time], that mine would never have been opened" and allowed to operate. Bell had done some contract work for Pike River Coal while the mine was being developed, and when he heard in late 2008 about underground gas ignitions, he urged the Department of Labour to shut the mine down until it was made safe.

Allan Dixon (Photo supplied by Gordon Dixon)

The state regulator took no action.

Workers at Pike River were under immense pressure to work long hours extracting coal, to satisfy the mine's shareholders. Gordon said his brother would "come home and just go to sleep because he was that exhausted." The poorly ventilated atmosphere made him, and other miners, feel sick.

Workers who spoke out about unsafe practices were ignored or told to shut up. When Allan injured his knee in the mine, he was told to return to work before it had healed or be sacked. "The surgeon actually said: 'Don't go back to work because your knee isn't right.' He was limping like hell," Gordon said. The company, however, refused to give Allan any more time off.

On the day of the explosion, Allan "wasn't supposed to be there. He was supposed to be on a course in Greymouth to get his deputy's ticket renewed." Management intervened and insisted that he had to go down the mine.

Gordon did not believe the claims made by police that all 29 workers died in the first explosion on November 19. He said Allan telephoned his partner Robyn from inside the mine after the explosion, leaving a message on her mobile phone. As *The Australian* newspaper reported, the message was something brief like "I love you."

Police initially dismissed the message, telling the media it was not from Allan Dixon, but Gordon said police eventually admitted, about a year ago, that there are phone records showing a call was made from inside the mine. "They weren't happy about it, and they've kept very, very quiet about it. I've asked for copies of the evidence and they said no," he said.

This was part of a pattern of mistreatment of the Pike River families under successive governments. Gordon recounted an exchange he had during a meeting with former Prime Minister John Key: "I said to John Key one day: 'What would you do if that was your son down there?' He said: 'I would try and get him out.' I said: 'Exactly, and what are you doing? Nothing.' He said: 'I don't have to listen to this,' and he just wandered away."

Gordon concluded that, as far as the government was concerned, "we're nothing, in the end. We're just the ones who have been fighting to get our loved ones out of the mine. They're not worrying about us; we're just a number to them."

Government lawyers announced in court in December 2013 that they were dropping charges against chief executive Peter Whittall, for breaches of health and safety laws, in exchange for an unsolicited payment to the families. Gordon Dixon was among several family members who denounced the backroom deal: "I stood up and said, 'This is blood money!' I was told by the judge to sit down, or I'd be taken out of court. We weren't allowed to speak, just to sit there and listen. That was really, really hard."

Police dropped their initial investigation into the disaster in mid-2013, saying that they could not charge anyone without establishing the precise cause of the explosion, despite ample evidence against the company from the royal commission. Given this record, Gordon was not optimistic that prosecutions would result from the present police investigation.

Son of disaster victim denounces lack of accountability
March 28, 2022

The WSWS spoke with Ben Joynson, whose father William died at Pike River. Ben, who was 10-years-old at the time of the disaster, spoke about the trauma that the victims' families have endured for more than 11 years—made worse by the fact that no one has been held accountable for the extremely unsafe conditions at Pike River.

Ben recalled how, for days following the first explosion, the families were told by the company that it was believed the men "were still alive, and they knew how to get them out and they were going to get them out." These hopes were shattered when families were told there had been a second explosion, and that the men were all dead. "When mum came home and told us, she broke down," Ben said.

A few years later, Ben experienced serious health problems as a result of post-traumatic stress. "I suffered a rupture in the optic nerve of my left eye, which is an injury that only happens to people in their 50s and 60s who have had heart attacks or strokes." Ben was one of the youngest Australians to experience such an injury. He also suffered from epilepsy and severe anxiety.

He emphasised that the decision not to issue any charges "caused a lot of pain and a lot of heartache" for the families. Like other family members, Ben believed that the unsolicited payment from Pike River management, in exchange for the charges being dropped, was unjust and was "blood money."

William Joynson, who died at the age of 49, had moved his family from Queensland, Australia to work at Pike River. He had a 17-year history working in underground mines, making him one of Pike River's most experienced workers. Ben said, "he was considered a very valuable team member in any workplace that he was in, because he was a man of diligence, honesty, integrity, and he was just a damn good worker."

William had concerns about safety issues, including the gas levels at Pike River, and Ben said he confronted management shortly before the disaster. Ben did not know what was said, but his father "would have had to have been incredibly upset about something to actually go to management, because in 17 years of working he had never done that."

William had spoken about his fears that he would not live to the age of 50. Journalist Rebecca Macfie relates in *Tragedy at Pike River Mine* that, days before the disaster, Kim had urged her husband to walk away because she feared for his safety.[46] Ben told the WSWS that his father "said he wanted to be there for his co-workers," but was planning to resign. The family were going to return to Australia in 2011.

The morning of the explosion, Ben said, "Dad came into my room and woke me up and said: whatever happens, look after your mum, look after your brother, make sure that they are looked after, just in case something happened to him."

Ben had a mixed reaction to the government's decision to walk away without exploring the mine workings. On the one hand, he said it was good that the investigation was ending because he felt tired of dealing with the ongoing media coverage and public discussion of Pike River, year after year. "It is quite detrimental to people's mental health," he said.

He added that the government has said the mine workings are not safe to enter. The WSWS explained that mining experts, including former chief inspector of mines Tony Forster, outlined last year how the re-entry could be conducted safely, but their plan was rejected by Minister Little.

Ben said, "I can also see the negative impact of stopping [the underground investigation]: we will never know what actually happened." He added that it "makes no sense" that police dug boreholes into the mine workings to search for evidence only after the mine had been sealed. He pointed out that this could

---

46. *Tragedy at Pike River Mine*, p165-166.

have been done years ago, "it didn't need to wait over a decade." He did not understand why the boreholes have now been blocked, "because you would think they would need to reuse them at some point."

The police borehole drilling operation was ended after only six sets of probable human remains were found, and two more "possible" bodies.

Asked whether he believed there had been a cover-up of the disaster, Ben said, "It does feel like a cover-up, it does feel like they're trying to hide something." He was not optimistic that the police investigation would result in prosecutions, saying that after more than a decade, "there should have been an answer by now, there should have been someone held accountable."

He said he thought the case would be dropped and Pike River would be "left to rot," but it would be remembered as an example of how not to run a mining company.

At the end of March 2022, the Pike River Recovery Agency handed over the mine site to the Department of Conservation, which is incorporating the mine portal into a new public walking track. The PRRA is to be disestablished at the end of June 2022.

Lessons of the 1994 Moura disaster in Australia

Terry Cook, a WSWS writer and long-standing member of the Socialist Equality Party (Australia) delivered this speech at the Socialist Equality Group's May 8, 2021, webinar.

Dear friends and comrades,

When I first heard the news of the Pike River mine disaster, my mind raced back over the many similar deadly mining incidents in Australia that I have been assigned by the party to cover to establish the truth and alert the international working class.

The April 20 statement for this meeting makes the salient point that the Pike River disaster "was not a random accident but the outcome of deliberate decisions to place production ahead of workers' safety."

This is incontestable. It is certainly true of the string of fatalities and life-threatening incidents across the Australian coal mining sector that our party has investigated to expose the cover up attempts of the official inquiries initiated by various governments in the wake of such disasters.

Among the many tragedies, the one especially burned into my memory is the explosion at the BHP No.2 Mine on August 7, 1994 in Moura, Central Queensland, which claimed the lives of 11 workers. To this day, the bodies of these men remain entombed underground after the company sealed the mine in the wake of a second explosion. The 1994 disaster was one of three that occurred in Moura in less than 20 years resulting, collectively, in the deaths of 36 workers.

The memory of 1994 remains so vivid because as part of our party's investigation I spent time in Moura, came to know the victims' families and witnessed first-hand their heart-breaking anguish over the loss of their loved ones during the interviews that I conducted with them in their homes.

However, this anguish was accompanied by growing anger over the utter contempt shown towards them by the company and the Queensland state Labor government of Premier Wayne Goss. In the wake of the disaster, Goss initiated a Mine Wardens Inquiry in a bid to contain the widespread outrage that erupted across mining communities. The purpose of this inquiry was not to establish the truth, but to whitewash the company and the government of responsibility.

The families' anger later extended to include the Construction Forestry, Mining and Energy Union (CFMEU). Its role in creating the conditions for the disaster became increasingly clear as miners began to speak out, encouraged to a large extent by our party's investigation and intervention.

Terry Cook with Leanne Dullahide, Rosemary Hogarth and Rosemary's daughter Brandy and grandchild. Dullahide and Hogarth both lost their husbands in the 1994 Moura explosion. (Death Underground, *Labour Press Books, 1996*)

In the immediate wake of the Moura disaster, the union had rushed to shield BHP from criticism, portraying it in the media as a "caring company." It backed the fraudulent inquiry and, in an attempt to give it legitimacy, the union's Queensland district secretary Peter Neilson served on its board.

The inquiry was forced to acknowledge that BHP was responsible for the miners' deaths, having sent them underground to continue production while knowing a highly dangerous and unstable situation existed. But it still recommended that no charges be brought against the company or any of its managers or executives.

I note that George Mason, who held management positions at the Moura mine during the disasters in 1986 and 1994, was recruited by Pike River Coal in 2010. In 1994, he had instructed his undermanager at Moura not to inform workers of the dangerous build-up of gas in a sealed panel next to where they were working.

It also became clear that the CFMEU was fully aware of the dangerous conditions in the mine prior to the explosion, including the presence of explosive levels of methane, because the union had been informed by its own members. Criminally, it did nothing to prevent workers entering the mine.

After the recommendation for no charges was announced, management and the union representatives at the inquiry shook hands and congratulated each on the outcome while the miners' families looked on in utter dismay.

I wrote at the time that this recommendation "was a green light to the mining companies that they could continue to kill and maim, with impunity."

Tragically, this prediction has been borne out by the plethora of mining deaths and shocking injuries that have occurred across the sector ever since.

This included the deaths of four miners at the Wallsend Coal Company's Gretley mine in New South Wales in 1996. They drowned after the machine they were operating cut into an adjacent disused mine shaft releasing a powerful inrush of water.

Again, despite evidence that standard precautionary measures, such as forward drilling, were not undertaken by the company, because this would have cut into production time and profit, the state Labor government's judicial inquiry into the incident made no recommendation for criminal charges against the mine's owners or operators. The mining union president at the time, John Maitland, cynically hailed this outcome as "another very significant day in the history of health and safety in the mining industry."

Over the past months, our party has been closely following the Board of Inquiry into the explosion at Anglo American's underground Grosvenor Mine in Central Queensland. This occurred on May 6 last year and left five workers with horrific injuries.

The inquiry was initiated by the Queensland Labor government for the same reasons as the 1994 Moura inquiry—to contain public anger that had already been generated by a spate of fatalities across the state's mines and to gain time to organise a cover to get the government and company off the hook.

This agenda became evident as early as last August when Anglo American managers refused to testify to the inquiry on the grounds of self-incrimination—a move that was supported by the state government. The inquiry's chairman, retired district judge Terry Martin, admitted that Anglo's refusal would "seriously compromise the inquiry and its ability to ever establish the cause of the Grosvenor Mine disaster."

The mining union, anxious to prevent any genuine probing of its own complicity in undermining safety across the industry, has backed this inquiry every step of the way, declaring last year that it was "an opportunity for a thorough, wide-ranging and independent examination of the shocking events."

In sharp contrast, injured miner Wayne Sellars, clearly determined that those responsible be held accountable, courageously gave evidence pointing to the extremely precarious conditions in the mine in the weeks leading up to the explosion, including the high presence of methane gas.[47]

To prevent further deaths and injuries, mine workers need to take matters into their own hands. This requires the establishment of rank-and-file committees completely independent of the corporatist trade unions to oversee and enforce workplace safety and to organise a unified industrial and political campaign in defence of workers' conditions.

The central lesson to be drawn from the years of bitter experiences is that the present system based on private ownership and profit is completely incompatible with even the most basic requirements of the health and safety of working people. This raises before miners and the entire working class the urgent

---

47. On February 22, 2022, Work Health and Safety Prosecutor Aaron Guilfoyle confirmed no one would be prosecuted: https://www.wsws.org/en/articles/2022/03/15/gros-m15.html

need for economic life to be reorganised on entirely different priorities—to meet social needs, not corporate profits.

The mines and major industries must be placed under public ownership and the democratic control of the working class so that production can be organised on the basis of safe and rational planning. This is the socialist program that is fought for by our parties in Australia, New Zealand and internationally.

Ten years after Christchurch earthquake, no justice for victims of building collapse

February 22, 2021

Today marks ten years since the February 22, 2011, Christchurch earthquake, which killed 185 people. Thousands of buildings were destroyed or severely damaged, and entire suburbs in the city's working-class east, an area once home to 10,000 people, were left uninhabitable and eventually abandoned, with the houses demolished.

Thousands of homeowners spent years fighting with private insurers and government agencies for their properties to be repaired or rebuilt. Some have still not received any pay-outs, one decade after the disaster.

The CTV building in 2004 (Photo by Phillip Pearson via Wikipedia, CC BY-SA 2.0, Cropped); *Ruins of the building, on February 24, 2011* (Photo by Gabriel, CC BY 2.0 via Wikimedia Commons, Cropped).

The death toll was not simply the product of an unavoidable natural disaster. Nearly two thirds of the lives lost, 115 people, were in the CTV (Canterbury Television) Building, which collapsed in seconds due to its extremely unsafe design. New Zealand is well-known for its frequent earthquakes, yet thousands of buildings are not constructed to withstand a severe shake, due to decades of deregulation and lack of government oversight.

The CTV victims included medical centre workers and Canterbury Television staff, as well as teachers and 64 foreign students at the King's Education language school, from Japan, China, the Philippines, Thailand, and South Korea.

The previous National Party government, the present Labour Party government, the police, and Crown Law (the state's senior solicitors), have all worked to prevent anyone being held accountable for the collapse.

Successive councils and governments themselves bear responsibility for creating the deregulated environment that inevitably leads to such tragedies. Beginning with the 1980s Labour government, both major parties have gutted safety standards across mining, construction, and other industries, allowing "self-regulation" by businesses.

A royal commission of inquiry in 2012 found that "the building permit should not have been issued" by Christchurch City Council in 1986, due to serious design deficiencies. And there were further inadequacies in the construction. Dr. Alan Reay, whose firm was in charge of construction, employed an unqualified engineer, David Harding, who had never worked on a multi-storey building before, and was not supervised by Reay.

Among other findings, the commission noted that there were "major weaknesses in all of the beam-column joints" and "the connections between the floor slabs and the north wall complex did not comply with basic engineering principles." But the commission had no power to hold anyone accountable.

Police began a criminal investigation in 2014 and hired engineering firm Beca, which produced a lengthy report identifying numerous design failures. In May 2017, police finally concluded their investigation and recommended prosecuting both Reay and Harding for manslaughter. However, the government's deputy solicitor-general, Brendan Horsley, intervened and argued that charges not be laid. On November 30, 2017, police announced that there would be no prosecution.

University of Canterbury engineering professor Maan Alkaisi, whose wife, doctor Maysoon Abbas, died in the building, is a spokesman for the CTV

Families Group, which continues to demand justice for the victims.

Alkaisi told the *World Socialist Web Site* that Horsley made the "outrageous" argument that there was no "public interest" in prosecuting anyone, and that a trial would cost millions of dollars. "So the lives of 115 people is not worth a trial, because it's too costly for him." Despite a mountain of evidence that the building was a death trap, Horsley also argued that there was "no major departure from normal practice" in the building's design.

Alkaisi pointed out that multiple investigations had identified more than 300 structural flaws in the building, "yet Mr Horsley ignored all this and he reckons that he knows more than all those experts in the field."

In a 2019 letter to Japanese victims' families, Horsley added, as an additional reason for not laying charges, that Reay was a man of "good character."

Alkaisi explained: "What we wanted was a trial. Let everybody come, let all the evidence be examined and cross-examined. Let [Reay] defend himself according to the rule of law. They don't want that. They want to go behind doors, take decisions, and nobody knows exactly how they reach those decisions."

Family members met with Horsley, police officials, and other representatives from Crown Law in December 2017. When Alkaisi asked questions about the abandonment of criminal charges, Horsley replied, "You are baying for blood." Another family member replied that this was not true, that the families wanted justice and to make sure such a disaster never happened again.

"This is Mr Horsley's mindset; he thought that we are baying for blood, whereas Alan Reay is a good character that we are chasing. So he was extremely biased," Alkaisi said.

Reay had at least two opportunities to rectify the building's design flaws: firstly, when a council inspector raised concerns in 1986, Reay did not change anything, but persuaded the council to issue a building permit. Then, in 1990, the flaws were again identified during the sale of the building, and Reay only ordered some minor work, which failed to fix them.

"The reason he did not do any remedy was because it will affect his reputation and it will involve him paying some money," Alkaisi said. "This is what really hurt us. It's for money that we lost all those people, for a few thousand dollars, that's all he was saving. It would not be millions to make the design a bit better, with a better beam column joint, with better connection between the slab floors and the main north wall. That would have saved the whole building."

Alan Reay and his wife remain major players in the construction industry. Their firm, Engenium (formerly Alan Reay Consultants Ltd), is involved in numerous public and private projects, including a $200 million apartment and retail complex in Epsom, Auckland. Alkaisi said, "I've been told many times: he is influential. So basically, if a person has money and contacts, he is above the law."

Brendan Horsley, meanwhile, was promoted last year by the Labour Party-led government to the job of Inspector-General of Intelligence and Security, one of the most sensitive positions in the state apparatus, overseeing the country's two spy agencies.

Prime Minister Ardern has rejected the CTV Families Group's request to appoint independent judges to investigate the police decision not to lay any charges. Ardern and other government ministers have refused to speak with the families about their case.

In December 2020, Alkaisi announced that the families would make a formal submission to the United Nations, alleging discrimination against them by the government. He told the WSWS they would "list all the mistreatment and all the injustice that we suffered in the last 10 years. They want to cover up, I want the entire world to know what happened."

Alkaisi concluded that politicians "have zero empathy for people" and only care about what will help them in the next election. "They want victims to be perceived as weak, crying, and just to move on, and believe anything they tell you. All their support is giving you a tissue to dry your tears."

Anita Stewart, whose brother Andrew Bishop died in the CTV Building, aged 33, told the WSWS: "I'm frustrated at the lack of justice. Wouldn't anyone be?" She noted that Reay's company "still rakes in millions of dollars and provides the owner with the lavish lifestyle that the deceased occupants of the CTV building couldn't even continue dreaming of."

Andrew worked for CTV as a cameraman and was a volunteer for Sumner Lifeboat, a maritime search and rescue operation. "I wish my brother wasn't a victim of the CTV Building. He died doing the job he lived for and with colleagues he called friends and family," Anita said. "It often feels like nobody seems to care anymore except our grief-stricken group. The more support our group receives, the stronger our foundation will be to fight for the justice that our loved ones deserve."

The appalling situation facing the CTV families is comparable to the decade-long fight for justice by the families of the 29 men who died in the Pike River disaster. "We share similar experiences, similar concerns, similar injustice," Alkaisi said.

Both cases, and many others internationally, like the official response to the 2017 Grenfell Tower fire in London, which killed 72 people, are examples of class justice.[48] The legal system is rigged in favour of rich and well-connected individuals and companies, who are shielded from accountability. The preventable tragedies in Christchurch and at Pike River, like the millions of needless deaths worldwide from the coronavirus pandemic, are the outcome of an economic system, capitalism, which places profit ahead of workers' safety and their lives.

Billions of dollars are urgently needed to strengthen and reconstruct buildings throughout the country to prepare them against natural disasters. This, in turn, requires a struggle for the socialist reorganisation of society, to place the resources of the banks and major industries under public ownership and democratic workers' control, to be used in the interests of human need.

---

48. See: "Four years after Grenfell, millions live and work in unsafe buildings as the criminals remain at large," June 15, 2021, https://www.wsws.org/en/articles/2021/06/16/gren-j16.html.

Appendix A: E tū union supports Pike River re-entry being aborted

This statement by E tū national secretary Bill Newson was emailed to Tom Peters on May 5, 2021, in response to the question: "Does E tū support the government's position that there is not enough money to continue the underground investigation of Pike River mine beyond the roof-fall?"

E tū consistently advocated for a re-entry of the Pike River mine up to the end of the drift to the point of the rockfall that has closed off the main mine shaft.

We supported the families and our mining members who needed to know whether any of the 'Pike 29' may have made it out of the main mine shaft and into the drift on the day of the disaster, and to ascertain any other relevant evidence.

E tū has balanced this with the health and safety of those doing the work to undertake the re-entry. Mining safety advice has been that safe re-entry up to the end of the drift was difficult but feasible.

We thank the government for undertaking that re-entry and to persevering to the end of the drift, and we thank the workers who did it.

The rockfall blocking off the main mine is substantial and we have been advised that overcoming that obstacle is a considerably more complex and dangerous challenge under mining regulations.

We know, to the great cost of the 'Pike 29' that it is a dangerous methane mine and that the logistics of gaining entry to that mine are considerably greater than gaining entry to the drift.

E tū's position is that we are satisfied that the government has kept its promise to re-enter the drift and supports the government's position regarding not re-entering the main mine.

However, should the government decide to undertake a further feasibility study to go further, E tū would be of any assistance that we may be able to provide.

Appendix B: Mine workers support the Pike River families

Between May and August 2021, the WSWS published nearly 100 letters from readers in New Zealand and internationally, supporting the fight by the majority of the Pike River families for a manned investigation of the mine workings. This selection is from miners and retired miners in the UK and Australia.

Malcolm Bray, UK:

Firstly, I would like to express my heartfelt condolences to the families who lost their loved ones at the Pike River mine in New Zealand on that terrible day.

As a former coal miner, I fully understand the dangers of working underground. Where I live in Barnsley, South Yorkshire, was the heart of the former mining industry in Britain.

The disaster at the Pike River mine was an absolute disgrace, considering the developments in mining technology, from advanced gas detectors and even miners' safety lamps that have been a reliable gas detector for many years in the mining industry, to the massive fans that are used to circulate fresh air around the mine. These types of disasters are entirely preventable if the mine owners utilised this technology properly rather than prioritising profits. That is why the Labour-Green government is keen to seal off the mine, denying these workers the dignity of a funeral and burying the evidence which would show the culpability of the company.

I fully support a full investigation into the deaths of the 29 miners at Pike River. However, this must not be left to the powers that be. We know the outcome would only lead at most to a slapped wrist fine and coverup. The families need answers, which would and should lead to the rightful prosecution of the company and all those responsible.

I went through the Miners' Strike of 1984-5. We were savagely attacked by the Tory government led by Margaret Thatcher and the state. What we experienced was the full brutality of the British ruling class. The National Union of Mineworkers (NUM) under the left leadership of Stalinist Arthur Scargill was incapable of standing up for the rights of miners and their families—he claimed it was not a political struggle against the government, allowed the miners to be isolated and put forward economic protectionism, pitting miners here against their class brothers internationally.

What I came to realise is workers cannot find justice within a system which only cares about profits over the lives and safety of workers. This has clearly been shown and highlighted during the pandemic.

Workers have been treated with indifference and contempt, everything is to suit the profit aspirations of the rich. The working class throughout the world is one class and must be united as one class. When the working class realise that, there will be no holding them back. Together, we can win everything. Nothing for the working class can be won through a national perspective and that's why the miners' strike in 1984-85 failed despite its militancy. Many workers around the world have suffered the same fate since.

British miners facing police during the 1984-1985 strike.
(Source: *Fourth International*, Volume 13 No. 1)

The struggles of workers are linked by the world crisis of capitalism. All the struggles must be joined, whether it's workers on strike, opposition to war and social inequality and defence of basic rights against the attempts to divide along national and racial lines. If workers are isolated, then it can only lead to one conclusion: injustice and defeat.

The bereaved families of the Pike River mine in New Zealand must seek international support. The campaign by the WSWS is doing this, in the process of building international rank and file committees. I believe this is the only way forward for all workers the world over. I fully support your campaign for justice and to hold those criminally responsible to account.

The "Miners Strike 1984-85" Facebook page is promoting your heroic stand and sharing coverage from the WSWS to bring news of your struggle to as wide an audience as we can.

Raymond Purcell, UK:
Yet again the mining community has been let down by a government that was formed originally on the backs of many miners to protect workers' rights. This government should hang its head in shame for not carrying out a full and sensitive inquiry into the deaths of hard-working miners in this terrible disaster. Just why a full forensic investigation is not going ahead is beyond me as this would give peace to the families and real closure to a Labour government and not a cover up as this seems in my opinion to be.

I worked as a coal miner for 23 years at Wearmouth colliery Sunderland UK. Our mine was worked for many miles under the North Sea, which took the lives of many people. As with all mining this is an extremely dangerous occupation which we all knew. But this is what makes coal miners a remarkable group of men—we all know the dangers but we still want and deserve a safe environment to do our job. When this safety stops and a tragedy happens then a full and honest inquiry is needed to prevent another man's life being taken in a similar way. So please do the right thing.

Mick Hutchinson, retired miner from Yorkshire coalfield, UK:
It stinks to think they could be so close to their loved ones and again it all comes down to money. Let me say this: money should never come into this. We all know that their loved ones have died. So get on with the recovery and bring their loved ones home so they can say their last goodbyes, for god's sake.

Charlie Seeney, ex-miner at Moura Mine, Australia:
Put the blame where it should be, at the company's feet. Greed should never overshadow safety. 29 Good Men lost their lives at Pike River, justice should be served. I live in a town where there have been three major mine disasters and the look of despair is still on some faces. I am truly sorry this has happened to your community. My heart goes out to the families of men taken too soon.

I don't understand why the mine was allowed to operate with only one means of egress. This is mandatory in every mine as a safety precaution. Your ventilation people should have picked up on this and ceased production until it was rectified. By having this in place the rescue squad may have stood a chance of at least seeing what went wrong. The second means of egress should have been at or near the shaft fan, that way any falls in the drift would have been bypassed.

Anthony Byrne, Australia:
This was a crime, no doubt about it. As an underground miner for many years my heart goes out to the families.

Appendix C: More letters supporting the Pike River families

Taryn, New Zealand:
I support the push for the continued investigation into the mine to recover the truth and possibly any deceased. I believe it is important to know what happened to cause the explosion so this may be avoided in the future and better practices can be in place for future mining so this may never happen again. My partner worked underground at Pike and I know there were inadequate safety procedures and equipment and that incident reports were ignored and pushed aside. These people must be held accountable and not able to work in these positions again. I hope the mine is not sealed in these coming days and that we can get some answers.

Johannah Pollock, UK:
My friend's son is [a few metres] from where they have dug to so far. To stop now and leave any chance of justice buried is just cruel. They know the cost is less than what has been publicised and is a drop in the ocean for the government. What cost loved ones' peace of mind?

Lynette Stevens, New Zealand:
Our family completely supports Dean and Bernie and others who need justice! Our family lost our brother on a corporate farm in NZ exactly a year after the Pike disaster... we know what the fight against corruption is like... so our utmost respect to you all!

Peter Moore, New Zealand/Australia:
Well, maybe [Ardern] will seal her fate too, when the election comes around. To all those families, I believe you deserve better from your government, but that's what happens when those who are ultimately responsible for the safety of

mines, and by that I mean the law makers and enforcers, get to control the investigation and information. Bit like police investigating police. To all the families involved, you might never know the extent of the support you have around the world. I can assure you that, almost without exception, you have the support of every miner—surface, underground, coal and hard rock—and decent people everywhere.

Hassan, New Zealand:

I am just wondering, if any of the men who died in the mine was the son, father or brother of one of the high-ups, would this case have gotten to where it is today? Is human life so insignificant as long as it is not one of theirs?

Also, New Zealanders going silent about this case not being handled properly are a big accomplice to the criminals. Albert Einstein once said, "The world is a dangerous place, not because of those who do evil, but because of those who look on and do nothing." Each New Zealander should put themselves in the shoes of the Pike River Families and feel the pain. Hopefully this will get them to fight with the families for their simple and basic rights.

Heather Christiansen, New Zealand:

I support the Pike River families, at the very least they deserve a fair trial. This has been a joke on behalf of our government. Why enter and investigate now to get their hopes up, only to shut it down again before it's even started? All that hard work, sweat and tears, has just put them through more turmoil and pain. These families need justice and at least a proper answer to put this to rest.

They say it's unsafe to enter, yet people put their life at risk to save other people every day. If someone wants to do it, let them. If it costs too much, why start it in the first place? The government wastes millions every year on silly things like referendums, for example John Key wanting to change the NZ flag. That is the least of our worries. Likewise, the cannabis and end of life referendums. These are all just to keep us distracted from what's really going on in our country. I'm pleading for the investigation to continue, no one deserves to go to work to die and not to return home.

Warren Duzak, United States:
To the people of New Zealand,

The job of underground mining for many of us is beyond comprehension, going underground often before first light and not coming out until dark. Miners and their families deserve the utmost consideration and protection. The case of the New Zealand mine and deaths is outrageous and fills me with disgust.

As an American US Army veteran, former journalist and the son of a New York City Fireman, I am proud to add my name to the list of those calling for justice for these dead miner/comrades and their families.

Nuwan, construction worker in Colombo, Sri Lanka:
The dangerous circumstances in which the workers died in the Pike River accident are clear. Workers all over the world have been forced into such dangerous conditions to make a living. We ourselves have been pushed to work under difficult conditions, as the COVID-19 pandemic has been utilised to destroy jobs. Workloads are unbearable as the number of workers has been cut.

Work-related accidents are on the rise due to the cutting of costs for our physical security, as in the Pike River mine. Here, employers have stopped providing safety boots. Instead, only giving low-cost canvas boots.

For months, I have not been with my wife and son. In the name of protecting us from the pandemic, the company has confined us. The same capitalist policy of placing profits ahead of human lives is in operation, as at Pike River.

The *World Socialist Web Site*, compared to other media, is totally different. Other media does not inform us of news relevant to the working class, such as Pike River. The WSWS always speaks from the workers' side. Only the WSWS and the SEP oppose the government's "essential service orders" in Sri Lanka that forces us to work in unsafe conditions. Even though we thought

105

that the trade unions would oppose these orders, they capitulated without saying a single word. Through the WSWS, I learned that they did so because they have been transformed into the instruments of the capitalists.

It is clear why the trade unions do not come forward to defend the rights of the Pike River workers: they are on the side of the company. So, I express my support to the committee and campaign that has been formed by the Pike River families independently of the trade unions. Building such committees, and discussing the political issues they face, is crucial. [Abridged]

Rachel Raue, New Zealand:

I fully support the Pike River Families Committee in their demand for a thorough investigation into the disaster that killed their loved family members on November 19, 2010. Further to this, the company leaders responsible for this gross and fatal negligence must be prosecuted.

The Ardern Labour government has a responsibility to ensure the safety of all workers in New Zealand. Without transparency in this most important case, that will never be possible. Corporate greed will continue to see to it that the lives of workers are to put at risk to ensure profit margins are met.

While Andrew Little says the government's decision to cease a forensic investigation is due to prioritising "the living," the details of the cover-up suggest, if not blatantly reveal, that this is really about protecting big business. Protecting the working class of New Zealand does not appear to be a priority. Neither is compassion or closure for all the victims of the Pike River disaster, either living or deceased.

International mining experts are backing these New Zealand families. Yet, their own government is turning their back on them, denying the enforcement of justice while supporting the continued enactment of the capitalist agenda that puts profit over people and planet. [Abridged]

More statements of support can be found in the WSWS archive on Pike River:
https://www.wsws.org/en/topics/event/2010-pike-river-mine-disaster

Appendix D: UK mines rescue expert says sealing Pike River mine is "morally and professionally indefensible"

On July 24, 2021, the WSWS published the following letter, sent by UK mines rescue expert Brian Robinson earlier in the month to Pike River Recovery Agency (PRRA) chief executive Dave Gawn, opposing the decision to seal Pike River mine and abandon the underground investigation.

Robinson provided advice on the re-entry of Pike River mine for several years, including to the PRRA. He is a member of the Independent Technical Advisory Group (ITAG), led by Tony Forster, a former chief inspector of mines in New Zealand, the UK and New South Wales, Australia.

The ITAG released a plan in May showing how the mine workings could be safely re-entered. This was rejected by Minister Andrew Little. In December 2016, when Labour was the opposition in parliament, Little praised Forster, and described Robinson as "the United Kingdom's leading mines rescue expert."

To: Dave Gawn
CEO Pike River Recovery Agency

Dave, we met in Greymouth some 3 years ago. I'm one of the ITAG expert group advising the Pike River families that have put the Conceptual Main Fan Re-Entry plan together.

It is obviously a shock at this stage of the Drift re-entry project to suddenly see the plug pulled, the finances stopped, especially as (as far as the public are aware) almost nothing of significance has yet been achieved. I'm aware finance is not your sole responsibility, but falls with Minister Little, I'm hoping this note may find its way to him.

Some years ago Minister Little certainly gave me the impression that they (Labour), if elected, would stop at nothing to re-enter the mine to find the cause of the disaster and repatriate human remains to the families. Having been involved in several mines rescue and body recovery operations in the UK, I now find it incredulous that after more than 10 years, and after such an encouraging start in 2018, this has not yet happened at Pike River and not a single body has been recovered and returned. So for me there are many, many more significant reasons NOT to seal the drift at this point than there are any reasons (apparently other than financial) to seal it.

As unpaid independent mining professionals committed to supporting the families, we have worked on this project for years, many having followed it right from day one of the explosion, and find the current situation both morally and professionally indefensible. The police will find it practically impossible to even view evidence properly, let alone recover any via borehole and that's only if the boreholes land in the right place. If after 10 years the police have not remotely conducted their investigation (i.e. without the benefit of re-entry), have not yet secured the evidence to lay criminal charges, I believe sealing the Drift without further exploration beyond the roof fall cannot be justified on any grounds.

The one thing that the Drift recovery has proven is that the Agency have all the necessary skills and ability to re-enter the mine workings when the correct measures and precautions are taken. Your team of engineers have amply demonstrated they can dilute and control mine gases wherever they need to, ensuring safety of all personnel at all times.

The Conceptual Recovery Plan put together by the ITAG, presents a credible and technically feasible plan to go beyond the roof falls that is based on sound mining practice, and is a task that has been carried out many times without incident. As a mining operator, PRRA must, by law, already have ventilation PCPs [Principal Control Plans] and Ground Control PHMPs [Principal Hazard Management Plans], so having demonstrated what they can safely achieve, to claim that it would take 8 months to plan the job frankly lacks credibility.

The ITAG group is an eminent group of worldwide, very experienced

Mining Engineers and mine safety practitioners. Most of the ITAG have at some time or other taken part in similar tasks within mines just for production reasons, let alone to gain evidence or recover remains, and in far shorter time frames and cost.

In summary, I firmly believe that the Agency should not seal the drift until the police have concluded their investigation fully, recovered sufficient evidence with criminal charges being laid, and the possibility of human remains being found.

Otherwise, $NZ50 million has been wasted. Any independent analysis would conclude that there are just too many negatives associated with sealing the mine permanently at this critical time.

Appendix E: Mine disaster inquiry whitewashes government
November 10, 2012

The National Party government released the findings of its Royal Commission of Inquiry into the Pike River mine disaster on November 5.

Twenty-nine men died when a methane gas explosion ripped through the mine in November 2010. Their bodies have never been recovered. The Pike River disaster was a crime in which the entire New Zealand ruling elite—business leaders, wealthy shareholders, political parties, media and the unions—was culpable. It was the outcome of the decades-long assault on the conditions, jobs and basic rights of the working class, carried out in the name of the "free market" to achieve "international competitiveness."

Any serious examination of the real causes of the mine explosion would have exposed that the safety of miners is incompatible with the current socio-economic system, where everything, including human life, is subordinated to the drive to accumulate profit. The Royal Commission, however, was designed to produce the narrowest of conclusions, covering up the political and economic circumstances underpinning the tragedy.

The Commission's more than 400-page report, based on testimony from mining experts and workers, concluded that the tragedy "was preventable." It found that Pike River Coal's board of directors "did not... protect the workforce from harm" and was "distracted" by "financial and production pressures." Executive management created a "culture of production before safety... and as a result signs of the risk of an explosion were either not noticed or not responded to."

Pike River Coal (PRC) sacrificed workers' safety, and ultimately their lives, by speeding up production and failing to install adequate safety equipment. The company, which was heavily in debt to its investors, proceeded to mine with no suitable emergency exit, inadequate methane drainage and ventilation, and faulty gas sensors. Employees were offered a bonus of up to $13,000 to work in dangerous conditions and meet production targets.

The report stated: "There were numerous warnings of a potential catastrophe at Pike River... For months [workers] had reported incidents of excess methane (and many other health and safety problems). In the last 48 days before the explosion there were 21 reports of methane levels reaching explosive volumes, and 27 reports of lesser, but potentially dangerous, volumes. The reports of excess methane continued up to the very morning of the tragedy. The warnings were not heeded."

Summing up the Commission's report, Bernie Monk told the media: "It was all there and no one picked it up. To me, it was all greed." Nicholas Davidson QC, a lawyer for the families of the dead miners, said the findings made New Zealand's mining industry "look like a seriously Third World operation."

The report noted that the Department of Labour (DoL) received repeated warnings about breaches of safety regulations at the mine but did not shut it down. The state regulator had just two mining inspectors at the time of the tragedy. It was woefully under-resourced and unable to properly assess compliance with safety legislation. Since 1992, the DoL has been gutted by successive National and Labour Party governments. Its specialist mines' inspectorate was dismantled. The requirement for mines to have worker-elected check inspectors was abolished, meaning that workers on mine sites had no independent representative with whom they could raise safety concerns. The mining industry has effectively been allowed to self-regulate safety.

The government is using the Commission's report to cover up its own culpability and return to business as usual. Prime Minister John Key was forced to admit that PRC "put its profits and its production ahead of the safety and lives of those 29 workers," but there will be no criminal prosecution of any of the company's directors or senior managers.

So far, PRC and its CEO Peter Whittall have only been charged with health and safety violations. Whittall has pleaded not guilty to 12 charges and will reappear in court next year. Last month, the contractor VLI Drilling, which operated at the mine, was fined the negligible sum of $46,800 after pleading guilty to three similar charges. PRC's former CEO Gordon Ward and its board members, including Chairman John Dow, have not been charged with any offence.

The Royal Commission's terms of reference specifically excluded the possibility of criminal prosecutions. The report's preface stated that "its views and conclusions should not be interpreted as determining, or suggesting the determination of, criminal or civil liability of any person."

No one in the National government or the Labour Party will be held accountable for decades of removing "red tape" at the behest of big business, creating the deregulated environment that led to the disaster. In an empty gesture, Kate Wilkinson has resigned her position as Minister of Labour, while keeping her seat in cabinet. Key insisted in parliament that Wilkinson had not contributed to the disaster "through any action or inaction," but merely "happened to be the minister responsible at the time." He added that the Commission found that "primary" responsibility rested with the company, while the government only had "some" responsibility.

Labour and the Greens have criticised the National Party for refusing to strengthen mining regulations since winning the 2008 election. Their posturing is completely hypocritical. During nine years in office from 1999 to 2008, Labour did not restore the mines inspectorate or worker-elected check inspectors. It allowed Pike River mine to open in 2008, despite clear safety breaches, including the lack of a second egress.

The Commission has recommended several changes to regulations, including a new government agency to focus solely on health and safety, a requirement for underground mines "to have modern equipment and facilities", legislative changes to strengthen safety guidelines and qualifications so they are comparable to those in Australia, better coordination of emergency responses, and the return of check inspectors—although significantly the Commission refers to inspectors "appointed" by the union, rather than elected by workers.

The government has promised to implement the recommendations, but no timetable has been specified and there is no reason to believe that genuine improvements to safety will take place. Even as the Royal Commission was sitting, the government continued to downsize the DoL, with 58 staff made redundant. To further cut costs, the DoL has been merged into a new Ministry of Business, Innovation and Employment.

Workers can have no confidence that inspectors appointed by the EPMU will put safety ahead of profit. The EPMU, New Zealand's largest private sector union, functions as an adjunct of the corporations. It had about 70 members at Pike River, but never once took industrial action or criticised the company's safety violations, even after a group of miners spontaneously walked off the job to protest the lack of emergency equipment. After the explosion, the EPMU's then national secretary and Labour Party president Andrew Little defended the company and said he was not aware of any safety problems at the mine.

The recommendations have been greeted with jubilation by the media, including supposedly "left" commentators, and the unions. *New Zealand Herald* columnist Bryce Edwards wrote that the "neoliberal framework for regulation may have finally had its day." The erosion of safety standards, however, is not the outcome of mistaken "ideology." Everywhere in the world, mining companies, backed by governments and trade unions, seek to maintain their competitive edge by pushing up productivity and cutting costs at the expense of their workforce. The global race to the bottom has intensified since the 2008 financial crash.

The wave of mine disasters in recent years—including in China, Chile, South Africa, Mexico, the US and New Zealand—demonstrates above all the urgent need for a rebellion against the unions and the establishment of new organisations of workers, based on a unified international struggle against the profit system for socialism.

Appendix F: Pike River families make Supreme Court appeal

October 10, 2017

The Supreme Court in Wellington heard an appeal on October 5 by family members of some of the 29 men who died in the 2010 explosion at the remote Pike River Coal (PRC) mine. The families sought a judicial review of the government regulator WorkSafe's decision in 2013 to drop charges against PRC chief executive Peter Whittall.

In February, the Court of Appeal rejected the families' case. The five Supreme Court judges have not said when they will make a decision.

No one has been held accountable for the disaster despite a 2012 Royal Commission finding that it was entirely preventable and that PRC had prioritised production over safety. Government regulators allowed PRC to operate despite flagrant safety breaches, including no adequate emergency exit, and inadequate ventilation and methane gas monitoring.

In 2013, PRC was found guilty of safety breaches and ordered to pay $3.41 million in reparations, but the company was bankrupt and refused to pay. In December that year, WorkSafe reached a back-room deal with Whittall's lawyers to drop 12 health and safety charges against him in exchange for payment to the families by Whittall and other company directors of the $3.41 million.

Police also decided in July 2013 not to press any charges over the disaster. Earlier this year it emerged that police had suppressed video footage taken inside the mine, which proved it could be re-entered safely to gather evidence. The mine has never been re-entered and the 29 bodies have not been recovered.

The families' lawyer Nigel Hampton argued in the Supreme Court that the "bargain," made by WorkSafe and Whittall without the approval of the families, was "unprecedented, unprincipled and unlawful." He said it "sets a dangerous precedent" for wealthy individuals to be able to buy themselves out of prosecutions.

In response, WorkSafe's lawyer Aaron Martin declared there was no "improper bargain" because WorkSafe was not "benefiting" from the non-prosecution of Whittall. In fact, any trial would inevitably have exposed the regulator's failure to prevent the explosion and the role played by successive governments in deregulating safety in the mining industry.

Martin descended into semantic sophistry. He admitted that "there was an understanding" that WorkSafe would drop charges against Whittall in exchange for the payment to the families, but then added, "that doesn't mean there was a deal."

The lawyer said WorkSafe decided a prosecution of Whittall was "not in the public interest" because of "a range of factors," including the probability of a "long, costly trial," which would have covered material already examined by the Royal Commission. Under questioning, Martin admitted there was no evidence WorkSafe had considered dropping the charges prior to the offer of payment.

Anna Osborne, whose husband Milton died in Pike River, told the WSWS that the regulator's defence was "absolute nonsense." She described the Royal Commission as "a farce," adding, "I think it was done way too early. What came out of it was best guesses as to what happened and we've got no real answers and still no accountability. What I'd like to see is an independent inquiry to properly get to the bottom of it all."

Sonya Rockhouse, who lost her son Ben, said if the families succeed in their application for a judicial review it would be "a moral victory" against the government. She added, "There's a lot more we would like to happen. We'd like Whittall to be brought back; we'd like the charges to be reinstated. None of that realistically is going to happen."

Rockhouse said the families would continue to demand justice "because no one's been held to account, not one person." She pointed out that after 96 people were crushed to death in 1989 at the Hillsborough stadium in Britain, it took 28 years before any of the police officers whose actions led to the disaster were charged.

The families hope the next government will organise a manned re-entry of the drift tunnel that leads into the mine. Seven years after the disaster, the opposition Labour, Green and New Zealand First Parties have promised to carry out a re-entry. Following the inconclusive election result on September 23, NZ First is currently deciding whether to form a coalition government with the National Party or the Labour-Greens bloc.

The government-owned company Solid Energy had wanted to permanently seal the mine entrance and only backed down earlier this year after months of protests by the families, which gained widespread public support.

Bernie Monk, whose son Michael died in the mine, told the WSWS that former Prime Minister John Key had made empty promises to re-enter the mine and retrieve the bodies. He said although many people were excited by the opposition parties' promises, "I'll never be excited till the job is finished."

Monk said the Pike River case "needs to be reopened, that's pretty obvious," and a re-entry of the mine "will bring a lot of evidence." He added that the families were still trying to obtain more information held by the police about the mine. "We're fighting for justice and accountability in New Zealand," he said.

None of the political parties has committed to reinstating charges or called for reopening the criminal investigation.

Monk said he had heard of recent attempts to cut staff at WorkSafe's specialist mining inspectorate, which was boosted following the Pike River disaster. He said a WorkSafe employee "came to me personally and asked me to do something about it. The disasters are going to start all over again."

Monk listed those he held responsible for the disaster in addition to the company: "The Department of Labour [now WorkSafe] cut back the inspectorate in 1992 under the National Party. The Labour Party didn't do anything [to reverse the cuts]; they were in power for three terms. They have honestly come forward and told us that. ... Mines Rescue did work at Pike River; they knew that that mine was unsafe. And number four is the unions, because they did not do their job."

The Engineering, Printing and Manufacturing Union, now called E tū, represented about half the workforce at Pike River. It worked hand-in-hand with the company. The union knew about safety breaches at the mine, which had prompted one walkout by workers in protest, but it never organised industrial action to ensure the mine was safe.

The union made no public statement about the unsafe conditions. Immediately after the explosion EPMU leader Andrew Little, who later became the Labour Party leader, defended Pike River Coal. He told the media there was "nothing unusual" about the mine and nothing that the union had been concerned about.

Index

119